Ethics in Management

Late S.A. Sherlekar

Retired Professor and Head of Business Management Department,
R.A. Podar College of Commerce,
Matunga, Mumbai - 400 019.

K.G. Bhat

M.Sc., M.A., MBA, LL.B., Ph.D.
Head, Content Development,
Banker's Quotient Academy, Mumbai - 400089.
email: kgbhat@bqlsg.com
Mob: 7045353049
Formerly,
Dy. General Manager & Principal,
Corporation Bank Staff Training College,
Mangalore - 575001.

Himalaya Publishing House

ISO 9001:2015 CERTIFIED

First Edition : 2015
Reprint : 2019
Reprint : 2023
Reprint : 2024
Reprint : 2026

Published by : Mrs. Meena Pandey
for **HIMALAYA PUBLISHING HOUSE PVT. LTD.,**
Vishal Industrial Estate, 1st Floor, Office No. 63/64,
Bhandup Village Road, Subhash Nagar (Opp. CEAT Tyres),
Nahur (W), Mumbai - 400 078. **Phone:** 022-35131464/65/66/67
E-mail: himpub@bharatmail.co.in; **Website:** www.himpub.com

Branch Offices :

New Delhi : "Pooja Apartments", 4-B, Murari Lal Street, Ansari Road, Darya Ganj, New Delhi - 110 002.
Phone: 011-23270392, 23278631; Fax: 011-23256286

Nagpur : Kundanlal Chandak Industrial Estate, Ghat Road, Nagpur - 440 018.
Mobile: 09325409992, 09325908881

Bengaluru : Plot No. 91-33, 2nd Main Road, Seshadripuram, Behind Nataraja Theatre, Bengaluru - 560 020.
Phone: 080-41138821; Mobile: 09379847017, 09379847005

Hyderabad : No. 3-4-184, Lingampally, Besides Raghavendra Swamy Matham, Kachiguda, Hyderabad - 500 027. Phone: 040-27560041, 27550139

Chennai : No. 34/44, Motilal Street, T. Nagar, Chennai - 600 017.
Mobile: 09380460419

Pune : "Laksha" Apartment, First Floor, No. 527, Mehunpura, Shaniwarpeth (Near Prabhat Theatre), Pune - 411 030.
Phone: 020-24496323, 24496333; Mobile: 09370579333

Cuttack : Plot No. 5F-755/4, Sector-9, CDA Markat Nagar, Cuttack - 753 014, Odisha. Mobile: 09338746007

Kolkata : 3, S.M. Bose Road, Near Gate No. 5, Agarpara Railway Station, North 24 Parganas, West Bengal - 700 109. Mobile: 09674536325

DTP by : Rakhi

Printed at : Trinity Academy, Delhi. On behalf of HPH.

PREFACE

Business environment in India is dynamic and complex. Post liberalization, some of the best practices in developed countries are followed by businesses in India. Business ethics, corporate social responsibility and governance are important components of emerging management thoughts being accepted by Indian Corporates.

Ethics reflects a society's notion about the rightness or wrongness of an act. Ethics also involves the evaluation and application of certain moral values that a society or culture has come to accept as its norms. Business ethics is the application of general ethical ideas to business behaviour. Ethics is a subject that deals with human beings. Society forms an opinion on the business based on the ethical behaviour of the managers of the business.

Corporate Social Responsibility is the continuing commitment by business to behave ethically and contribute to economic development while improving the quality of life of the workforce and their families as well as of the local community and society at large. Corporates use all the resources from the society for producing its products and services and depend on the society for earning the profits. Corporate is obliged to the society in which it operates. During the process of doing business, corporates cause damage to the environment, deplete the scarce resources. This necessitates, business firms a responsibility to share a part of its profits for improving the quality of life of the society by its direct intervention. Good corporates take proactive initiatives to return part of its gains by taking up good projects like development of villages, increasing hygine in rural areas by providing basic facilities, maintaining gardens, running schools, hospitals etc. to name a few.

Corporate governance is the other important management practice seriously advocated by the financial/capital market regulators and the government. A series of corporate scams and collapses in the late 1980s and early 1990s brought to the fore, inadequacy of the rules and regulations to curb unlawful and unfair practices of corporations. The collapse of markets during 2008 in developed countries reconfirmed that loopholes in the governance of corporates in general and financial system in particular. Major scams like UTI scam and Satyam fraud exposed the fragile governance practices in corporate world in India. Initiatives taken by regulators and governments of respective countries tried to strengthen the governance and brought transparency. These efforts are expected to increase the efficiency of capital market and enhance the ability of corporates to raise required capital for projects.

These three management thoughts, i.e., business ethics, corporate social responsibilities and corporate governance are interconnected closely and corporates have to voluntarily accept and follow the regulations.

This book is modeled to cover the three subjects at required rigour for postgraduate studies.

Originally written by Mr. S. A. Sherlekar, I have the good fortune to review the book to make it relevant to emerging business dynamics. The book has been chiseled to meet the syllabus of University and it is hoped that the students and other users will find the book current and useful.

My thanks are due to Himalaya Publishing House Pvt. Ltd. for bringing out the revised version in this form.

15th Jan, 2015

Head Content Development,
Banker's Quotient Academy,
4th Floor, Trade World,
Kamala Mill Compound,
S. B. Marg, Mumbai- 400 013.

Dr. K. Govinda Bhat

CONTENTS

This Chapter deals with:

- What is Management?
- Meaning of Management
- Concept of Management
- Importance of Management

INTRODUCTION

Management by materialism today is the handmaid of profit-making at any cost. Man in the term 'manager' stands nowhere. We have no human touch in management. We have loss of human values. Managers and leaders in any branch of human enterprise unfortunately are setting a bad example today before the people. The managers at all levels are expected to have strong and noble character based on basic human values. They must adopt means and ends or objectives based on ethical and moral values. But we have almost the reverse picture in our country and abroad. Under such circumstances, there is a crisis of confidence in management and labour. Workers are dehumanized and demoralized. Consumers are by-passed. Human welfare is sacrificed. Nature is ruthlessly exploited. The environment has pollution. Wealth is gained. The soul is lost.

As long as soul is defectively organized, there will be outward and inward unrest, disorder and breakdown even though you got rid of material poverty. Soulless management is unwanted.

Management has to rely on the development of heart and soul. We want management by consciousness, management by soul. Management must be value-driven. It must adopt holistic approach. A good man with a noble heart and soul makes a good and responsible worker and manager.

The value-oriented and holistic management will enable us to lead a much better life, much more qualitatively superior life. This will bring us greater happiness when it is really translated into societal benefit in the form of running an organization or in any other field of human activities.

When you bring that spiritual state of mind and combine it with knowledge, values and skills, the benefits to you and to the society are enormous.

Such management will help ordinary people to produce extraordinary results. Productivity of human capacity is much more important than plant capacity.

Under competitive economy and ever changing environment, the quality and performance of managers determine both the survival as well as success of any enterprise. A supply of capable management experts is a basic and critical resource without which economic advancement would soon be aborted or steriled.

Organizations are social devices to achieve some stated purpose efficiently through group means and are the result of interaction among people, and the need to achieve something with managerial leadership. Whenever and wherever a group is formed and a group activity is organized to achieve certain common goals, management is needed to lead, co-ordinate and integrate the individual activities of a group and secure teamwork to accomplish organizational goals. Competent managerial leadership alone can ensure effective group action in order to realize the planned group goals. In essence, management is a social function. It can take us from some condition we do not want to one that we want – by setting goals and integrating human and material resources to achieve those goals.

"The emergence of management as an essential, a distinct and leading social institution is a pivotal event in social history. Rarely, if ever, has a new basic institution, a new leading group, emerged as fast as has management since 1960. Rarely in human history has a new institution proved indispensable so quickly; and even less often has a new institution arrived with so little opposition, so little disturbance, so little controversy." – P. Drucker: The Practice of Management.

WHAT IS MANAGEMENT?

Management is an exercise in harmonizing men, money, machinery, materials and methods towards fulfilling of set objectives leading to human development, excellent performance, social benefit and global welfare. Man, a conscious being, remains the basic factor in any field of human endeavour.

One way to analyze management is to think in terms of what a manager does. Using this approach, we can arrive at the management process which describes the work of any manager. The management work can be divided into a few basic functions of management, viz.,

1. Planning
2. Organizing
3. Leading
4. Controlling

Planning is the determination of objectives and formulation of plans, strategies, programmes, policies, procedures and standards needed to achieve the desired organization objectives. To implement the plans, there must be some organization structure. The human and material resources or inputs are allocated to the various units and relationships are established among the sub-units. Organizing is the second function of manager. Organizing is the process of developing a structure among people functions, and physical facilities to execute the plans and achieve stated objectives. The third function of a manager is that of leading – stimulating and motivating people in the organization to undertake willingly the desired actions as per pre-determined plans and objectives. Motivation is an integral part of leadership to assure desired results. The fourth and final function of management is that of controlling to assure management-in-action as per plans and objectives. Controlling incorporates the establishment of standards, measurements and comparison of actual results against the standard, and necessary corrective action to remove deviations from the plan.

Management is a universal process in all organized activities. It is not merely restricted to factory, shop or office. It is an operative force in all complex organizations trying to achieve some stated objectives. Management is necessary for a business firm, government enterprises, education and health services, military organizations, trade associations and so on. Hence, management skills are transferable and a manager can successfully apply his knowledge and skill in a wide variety of enterprises. Of course, situational factors will influence the suitable combination of managerial skills. Experts agree that management is a distinct activity in any branch of collective human efforts. Similarly, all managerial functions are universal and all managers in any branch of business or non-business activities perform those typical functions of management cycle, viz., planning – organising – leading – controlling. "Management is a multi-purpose organ that manages a business, manages manager, and manages workers and work." – P. Drucker: "The Practice of Management."

Drucker stresses three jobs of management:

(i) Managing an organization

(ii) Managing a manager; and

(iii) Managing workers and work.

Even if one is omitted, we would not have management any more and we also would not have an enterprise. According to P. Drucker, it requires the manager to and harmonize three major functions of the enterprise. Hence, a manager is a dynamic and life giving element in every organization. Without efficient management, we cannot secure best allocation and utilization of human, material and financial resources.

"Management is decision-making." Decisions are necessary in all functional areas of any organization. Manager by profession is decision-maker. All managerial functions are discharged through decision-making. All human behaviour involves the problem of choice. The process of making selection is termed as decision-making. We have two distinct levels of activity in management:

1. co-ordination and
2. supervision.

The co-coordinative function is that of decision-making — the process of selecting an action from the alternative courses of action. Management in the co-ordination sense is the central concept of management theory. Decision-making is the core of the process of management. In short, decision-making pervades all managerial functions. This definition ignores the function of supervision and leadership.

"Management is the process of designing and maintaining an environment, working together in group to efficiently accomplish selected aims." – Koontz/Weinrich: Management.

According to this definition, management is an art of creating performance environment enabling the group to attain stated objectives and management is the body of organized knowledge, i.e., science which underlines the art. Creation of managerial environment for joint efforts of people working in an organization in order to accomplish planned objectives demands intelligent application of management knowledge to numerous and varied practical problems so that we can have the best results under the given situation or realities.

MEANING OF MANAGEMENT

Management is a social process. It is directly in charge of allocation, utilization and co-ordination of all human and material resources to be procured from the environment or the society. The environment provides these resources as inputs to an enterprise. Most of these resources are scarce and have alternative uses. Management has to evolve optimum combination of these resources or inputs. The resources are co-ordinated and integrated by the management through performing the typical managerial functions. These functions constitute the process of management. The basic resources are subjected to fundamental functions of management. Management process is necessary to determine the objectives and goals and to take appropriate action, i.e., implement the plan in order to accomplish the stated objectives. Controlling ensures performance as per plan and enables the management to remove the deviations, if any, between the actual results, and expected results. As people are our greatest resources, management has a special responsibility to create favourable work environment and ensure maximum employee morale and productivity. Hence, management has not only to manage the business but also to manage both managers and workers. Motivation and leadership are the two unique managerial functions or activities to ensure maximum use of human resources without sacrificing human welfare and human satisfaction. As a manager, you will be called upon to play different roles under different situations, such as planner, co-ordinator, leader, liaison (connecting link), monitor, spokesman, disseminator of information, risk bearer, resource allocator, negotiator, disturbance handler, resolver of interpersonal and interdepartmental conflicts, and so on. Classical or bureaucratic management is appropriate where the environment is relatively unchanging. Behavioural and organic management is appropriate where environment is dynamic and innovation and creativity are at a premium.

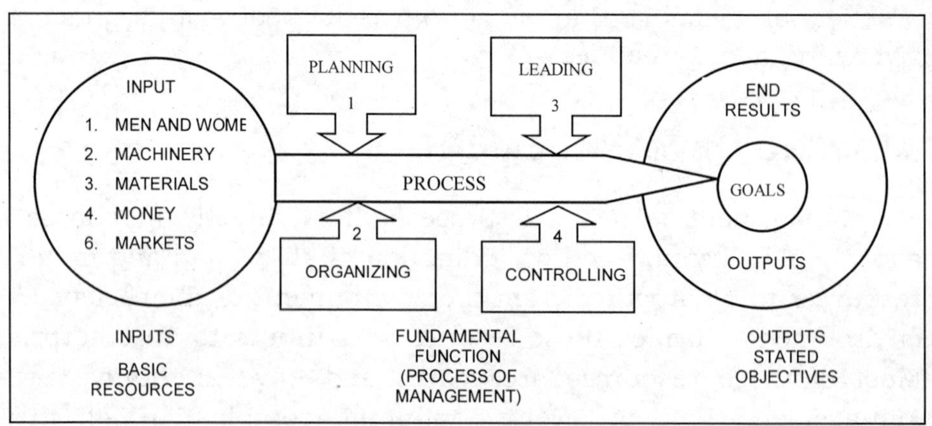

Figure 1.1: Graphic presentation of management process

CONCEPTS OF MANAGEMENT

Management is a central directing and controlling agency indispensable for any enterprise involving organized co-operation and requiring collective efforts to realise some common desired results or specific objectives. The group efforts in the pursuit of common goals and objectives require proper leadership which is provided by the management. Management has three distinct meanings.

1. **Management as a Process:** This describes an activity, which can be better described by the word managing. Under this concept, we consider activity by means of which scarce resources are combined to achieve given ends. Manager draws upon the basic resources which are called 6Ms — men, materials, machines, money, minutes and methods. These six resources are subjected to the management process which consists of typical elements of management or functions of management such as planning, organizing, motivating, leading and controlling of human efforts. Through these managerial functions or management process, we can have accomplishments of:

   - The right work
   - At the right place
   - At the right time and
   - With the right method

   From such managerial activities, we derive the expected results, viz., benefits and satisfactions in individuals, groups, enterprises as well as the society at large. Productivity of all resources in the final analysis depends upon the competency and ability of management of any enterprise to deliver the goods. Thus, management will convert disorganized resources of men, money, machines, etc. into useful enterprise. These resources are mobilized, co-ordinated. directed and controlled in such a manner that the enterprise would work towards the realization of common objectives. Management provides a dynamic force in getting any enterprise in useful activities. It makes significant social contributions, e.g., customer's needs are met, employees gain jobs and citizens enjoy higher standard of living. It assures economic growth free from pollution. Government would have income through variety of taxes. In short, management is an invigorating force bringing to life what would otherwise be only potentialities.

Mental poise and balanced temperament can be developed by building up strong character reflecting the basic human and ethical values. This state of mind is needed to cope with the inevitable stress and strain arising in your day-to-day life. Thus, when values and skills are combined by a manager and workers, the management of an organization will be much better. There would be smooth interaction with people. The management of stress will be easier. The quality of life and the quality of work would be enhanced. Mind-stilling exercises will also enrich life of an organization.

2. **Managers:** The term management may refer to those who are carrying on the activity of management, viz., the managers to manage an organization, who manage the managers and who manage the workers and the work. In a large organization, we have different levels of management. The top management, i.e., managerial agencies at the top is the governing board of directors, which is the supreme policy-making and decision-making authority, the managing director, the chief executive or the executive directors as the heads of major divisions. These constitute the top management. Then we have middle management group consisting of middle managers, i.e., departmental managers, and subordinate officers who work under the heads of the departments and who enjoy delegated authorities from their bosses. The flow of authority or power is always downward, flowing from the top to the bottom and this is brought about by proper delegation. Manager himself can do nothing. He cannot produce goods. He has to multiply his personality particularly in a big organization and this is done through delegation of authority. Hence, many a time, management is defined as that agency which

gets things done through and with other people. This definition points out the importance of delegation and motivation in management. This definition also implies decision-making process as an integral part of management. Delegation transfers steadily the decision-making power from the higher level to the lower level. Under the middle management group, we have lower level managers such as supervisors, foremen who are directly in charge of the operatives, i.e., rank and file of workers. Lower level managers, middle managers and top managers are many a time called management as distinguished from labour, viz., the operatives or workers. At present, greater empowerment of workers is also expected.

3. **Special Field of Study:** Profession, the third concept of management, points out that it is a body of knowledge about the activity of managing or the process of management and this body of knowledge is usually regarded as a special field of study, i.e., profession. The third concept of management as a profession is due to the managerial revolution which took place since 1960. In a joint stock company, there is complete separation of management from ownership. Shareholders are owners of the enterprise. They do not have management rights and we have a small body of executives representing professional managers to whom is entrusted the work of management. Under a corporate personality, management has emerged as a separate entity and it reveals the professional character of management, i.e., Management by Salaried Experts.

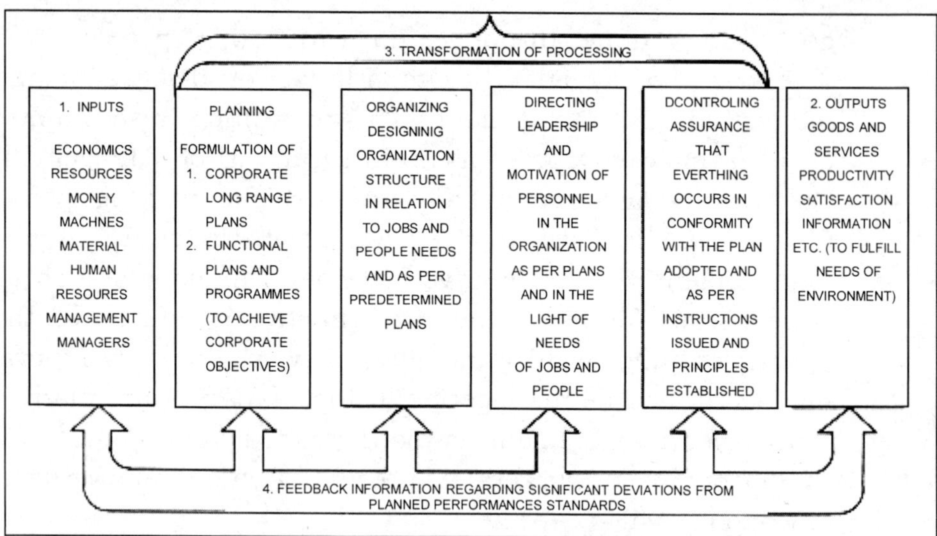

Figure 1.2: The total system covering: 1. Inputs or resources. 2. Outputs or produces and satisfactions. 3. Managerial process or functions for transforming inputs into outputs. 4. Control loop through feedback process assures cyclical or ongoing process of planning – action control in changing environmental or situation

- Planning denotes the determination of short to long range plans in order to achieve the objectives of organization. We have policies, procedures, programmes, schedules, rules and budgets.
- Organizing indicates the development of sound organization structure according to predetermined plans.
- Leading means stimulating and motivation of personnel of the organization according to predetermined plans.
- Controlling offers assurance that management-in-action is taking place as per plan.
- We have an ongoing cycle of planning-action-control replanning.
- Control function closes the system loop by providing adequate and accurate feedback of (significant deviations from planned performance in time. Feedback can affect the inputs or any of the managerial functions or the process so that deviations can be removed and goals can be accomplished. The measurement and comparison of actual with the standard and subsequent corrective action is referred as 'feedback.' An

arrangement in which the input depends on feedback from the output is known as a 'closed loop control system', or feedback control system.

- A system is a goal-oriented set of elements or subsystems whose sub-goals must be subordinated to the total system goals for optimization. A system has inputs, a processor, outputs and usually a feedback of information with subsequent corrective actions.

IMPORTANCE OF MANAGEMENT

At all levels of organization in any joint enterprise (requiring teamwork), managing is an essential input and it is said that anything minus management amounts to nothing. Management is the most critical asset for the success of any enterprise.

Management can deliver rising standards of living and standard of life to the society. It can offer enriched life to employees, consumers and citizens or members of a community. It assures smooth running of an enterprise. It is a powerful innovative force. It is the main determinant of our economic progress. It is the guide for our effective government. It can strengthen our national defence.

Specialists of economic development have pointed out to the governments of developing countries that even the most modern technology, best materials, resources and plant facilities, liberal and cheap finance may not be able to achieve stated objectives (industrial productivity and quality of working life) without effective and efficient management. The greatest obstacle and the limiting factor for undeveloped and developing countries is the quality of management. Competent managerial personnel was really responsible for the accelerated development and recovery of Germany and Japan after the World War II after 1950.

Good management is the only economic resource which can decide the extent of utilization of all other resources. It alone is responsible for the optimum utilization of available scarce resources.

Productivity of resources is the current burning problem in all countries. Problem of inflation and ever-growing consumer demand due to growth of population have created unique importance to productivity. Management is called upon to meet the challenge of productivity. Managers have to manage separately the productivity of all four key resources: capital, crucial physical resources, time and labour (skilled people, wisdom people, managerial and professional people). But what matters in the end is the total, overall productivity of an enterprise, e.g., factory, store bank, hospital, school, office and so on. Managers must commit themselves to accomplish steady increase in productivities of all resources particularly in turbulent and ever-changing environment.

Good management recognizes immense potential energy of human resources. Human resources are more productive than material resources. Good management brings out this potential energy. Good management is necessary in industry, commerce, agriculture, hospital, educational institution, sports, charitable institution, political bodies, trade unions and Government. In the field of co-operation, small and cottage industries, we need good management. Government is the greatest industrialist and greatest employer in India. Hence, management has gained greatest importance in all government branches of administration.

CHECK YOUR UNDERSTANDING

1. Discuss the definition and scope of management.
2. Discuss the nature and importance of management in modern organizations.
3. Explain the concept of management.
4. What is the importance of man in the management?
5. What are the steps/processes involved in management?
6. Bring out the concept of ethical management with suitable examples.

REFERENCES

1. Hicks and Gulleck: Management of Organizations.
2. Weihrich and H. Koontz: Management – A Global Perspective.
3. Drucker, P.: Practice of Management.
4. Chakraborthy, S.K.: Human Values for Management.
5. Raja, K.C.R.: Indian Ethos in Management, Somaiya Institute of Management.
6. Gupta, G.P.: Management by Conciseness

This Chapter deals with:

- Definition of Business Ethics
- Nature of Business Ethics
- Characteristics
- Ethical Theories
- Causes of Unethical Behaviour
- Ethical Abuses
- Work Ethics
- Code of Conduct
- Public Good

INTRODUCTION

In today's global competitive environment, people and businesses are expected to behave in an ethical manner and follow ethical standards of behaviour. These standards are dictated by ethical norms. Various ethical norms are commonly held by people around the world, such as those that condemn murder, theft, deceit, and so on. These norms are central to human existence and to life in society. However, there are norms that are viewed as ethical in one country and unethical in another country. The challenge is to behave in an ethical manner and follow the ethical standards as dictated by local norms. If businesses and people do not behave in an ethical manner, they may face negative consumer or public reactions and even government prosecution that can generate negative publicity and even litigation.

CONCEPT OF ETHICS

What is ethics? Ethics is the set of universally accepted moral principles and values that govern the behaviour of a person or group in terms of what is right and wrong. Ethics is concerned with how people think about and behave towards each other; how the consequences of their decisions and behaviour impact human life.

What is business ethics? Business ethics is about the rightness or the wrongness of business practices. Business ethics is guided by principles of commercial relationships and right and moral standards applied within an enterprise that indicate what is good and right for business.

Ethics is the basis for developing a system of morality and the moral laws that evolve from ethics. Morality is the activity that governs appropriate human conduct in a given culture. People's behaviour is guided by moral rules and obligations that show how to behave. People have many moral obligations in their lives. For example, it is a moral obligation to care for one's parents and children, and even to support one's country.

BUSINESS ETHICS – DEFINITION

Business ethics is the field of study dealing with right and wrong behaviour in the business world. Ethics takes on different meanings in different cultures, making it challenging to truly define business ethics in international markets. However, there are a number of actions that are almost universally considered unethical and for which numerous developed nations maintain criminal laws to prevent. Reviewing a few examples of ethics violations in the business world can help you to understand the kinds of things that are unacceptable in almost every culture.

"Business ethics", a subject that for years has been a low profile in business publications and business school curriculum, has suddenly gained status. The word 'ethics' was once considered irrelevant by corporate loyalists, but now it is increasingly seen as not only important but also critical to a company's success. The intensity of consumer movements and the rising levels of awareness among corporate stakeholders are making it difficult for corporates to get away with unethical business practices. Indian corporates have lately realized that integrity, transparency, and open communications are the new norms of the corporate world.

Ethics is a subject that deals with human beings. Humans by their nature are capable of judging between right and wrong, good and bad behaviour. Ethics is a normative science. The word normative implies a guide or control of action; so normative ethics tells us what we ought to do. Ethics deals with human conduct that is voluntary and not forced by any persons or circumstances.

Business can be defined as a primary economic institution through which people in modern societies carry on the task of producing and distributing goods and services. Business ethics refers to the application of ethical judgments to business activities. Business ethics concerns itself with what is right or wrong in the workplace. Business ethics can also be considered as an ethical analysis of business practices. Business ethics explains that business can generate profits even when being ethical. Due to expansion of business, the application of ethical practices and its implications has created a need for practicing business ethics. Today, much importance is being given to the application of ethical practices in business dealings and the ethical implications of business decisions.

At times, business finds it difficult to explain its actions on ethical ground. Any business, if it wants to survive and grow in the long run must strike a balance between its social obligations and economic objectives. These obligations may be complex and costly to discharge. But if the organization wants to be ethical, it has to discharge its social obligations towards the society. In concept, business ethics is the applied ethics discipline that addresses the moral features of commercial activity.

Business ethics can be defined as written and unwritten codes of principles and values that govern decisions and actions within a company. In the business world, the organization's culture sets standards for determining the difference between good and bad decision-making and behaviour. In the most basic terms, a definition for business ethics boils down to knowing the difference between right and wrong and choosing to do what is right. The phrase 'business ethics' can be used to describe the actions of individuals within an organization as well as the organization as a whole. A company's managers play an important role in establishing its ethical tone. If managers behave as if the only thing that matters is profit, employees are likely to act in a like manner. A company's leaders are responsible for setting standards for what is and is not acceptable employee behaviour. It's vital for managers to play an active role in creating a working environment where employees are encouraged and rewarded for acting in an ethical manner. Managers who want employees to behave ethically must exhibit ethical decision-making practices themselves. They have to remember that leading by example is the first step in fostering a culture of ethical behaviour in their companies. No matter what the formal policies say or what they are told to do, if employees see managers behaving unethically, they will believe that the company wants them to act in a like manner.

Business ethics is the behaviour that a business adheres to in its daily dealings with the world. The ethics of a particular business can be diverse. They apply not only to how the business interacts with the world at large, but also to their one-on-one dealings with a single customer. Many businesses have gained a bad reputation just by being in business. To some people, businesses are interested in making money, and that is the bottom line. It could be called capitalism in its purest form. Making money is not wrong in itself. It is the manner in which some businesses conduct themselves that brings up the question of ethical behaviour. Good business ethics should be a part of every business. There are many factors to consider. When a company does business with another that is considered unethical, does this make the first company unethical by association? Some people would say yes, the first business has a responsibility and it is now a link in the chain of unethical businesses. Many global businesses, including most of the major brands that the public use, can be seen not to think too highly of good business ethics.

Many major brands have been fined millions for breaking ethical business laws. Money is the major deciding factor. If a company does not adhere to business ethics and breaks the laws, they usually end up being fined. Many companies have broken anti-trust, ethical and environmental laws and received fines worth millions. The problem is that the amount of money these companies are making outweighs the fines applied. Billion dollar profits blind the companies to their lack of business ethics, and the dollar sign wins. A business may be a multi-million seller, but does it use good business ethics and do people care? There are popular soft drinks and fast food restaurants that have been fined time and time again for unethical behaviour. Business ethics should eliminate exploitation, from the sweat shop children who are making sneakers to the coffee serving staff who are being ripped off in wages.

NATURE OF BUSINESS ETHICS

Business ethics refers to the application of ethical principles of business. According to Velasquez, "Business ethics is a specialized study of moral right or wrong. It concentrates on moral standards as they apply to business policies, institutions and behaviour".

The main features of business ethics are as follows:

(i) Business ethics is applied ethics. It involves the application of what is good and right to business affairs.

(ii) Ethics is the study of morality just as chemistry is the study of the properties of chemical substances. However, ethics is not the same as morality. Ethics is a kind of investigation whereas morality is the subject matter of such investigation. Morality refers to the standards that an individual or group has about what is right and wrong. Honesty is good and dishonesty is bad is an example of moral standards. Ethics examines the moral standards of a group or society to determine whether these are reasonable or unreasonable.

Ethics is a normative study of morality. The normative study is an investigation that makes conclusions about what actions are right or wrong, good or evil. Sociology and Anthropology make a descriptive study of morality. A descriptive study is an investigation that develops accurate description of the moral standards of a particular culture. For example, sociologists ask "Do moralists believe that bribery is wrong?" On the other hand, ethicians ask "Is bribery wrong?". Thus, business ethics comprises not only the analysis of moral norms and values but also attempts to apply the conclusion of such analysis to business.

Three kinds of issues are investigated under business ethics. First are the systematic issues in which ethical questions are raised about the economic, political legal and social systems within which business enterprises operate. Second are the corporate issues wherein ethical questions are raised about the policies and practices of a particular business enterprise. Third are the individual issues wherein ethical questions are asked about the decisions, actions and characters of particular individuals within an enterprise.

Moral standards apply as much to corporations as to individuals. But a corporation being an artificial person, individuals who manage and control it are held responsible for its immoral decisions and actions.

CHARACTERISTICS

Ethicists have suggested five characteristics that highlight the nature of moral standards:

(i) Moral standards deal with matters that can seriously injure the society without them. For example, in every civilized society, theft, rape, murder, fraud and law-breaking is considered immoral because these cause serious injury humanity.

(ii) Moral standards are not created or changed by the decisions of any particular authority like legislature. The validity of these standards depends on the adequacy of the reasons that are taken to support and justify them. So long as the reasons are adequate, the standards remain valid.

(iii) Moral standards may, at times, come into conflict with self-interest. If a person has a moral obligation to do something, it has to be done, even if it causes harm to his self-interest. For example, Raja Harishchandra sacrificed his kingdom and family to uphold his high moral standards of truth and honesty. Moral standards are maintained not for the sake of reward but for the value attached to them. The values attached to a moral standard extend beyond personal interest to a universal standpoint.

(iv) Moral standards are based upon impartial consideration. These standards are evaluated not on the basis of who will benefit or who will be harmed. In morality, everyone's interest are impartially counted as equal.

Impartiality is, no doubt, one of the important characteristics of moral standards. But it is often balanced with some kind of partiality, particularly when it arises from legitimate caring for family members and friends. In such cases, preferential caring may be morally legitimate and perhaps even morally required. For instance, in the great epic Mahabharatha, Karna the great warrior sided with and fought for his benefactor friend Duryodhana who gave him succour and status.

(v) Moral standards are associated with special emotions and special vocabulary. For example, persons, adopting strict moral standards will feel 'ashamed' or 'guilty' of even thinking about going beyond moral standards. Even if they happen to do something 'wrong' against their moral standards, they will feel 'remorseful'. Such people will express their indignation or resentment towards those persons who are not living up to the moral standards.

ETHICAL THEORIES

It's difficult to say exactly what ethics is, but we can say that it involves a standard of what is right and wrong based on what people ought to do. This may include:

- Our obligation to society
- What benefits society rather than the individual
- Being fair to others

This seems rather vague. This is mostly because there is no specific definition for each standard that can be considered part of ethics, nor are there specific guidelines as to what standards even fall under the definition of ethics. We can, however, safely assume that most people in society think that things like rape, adultery, stealing and murder are wrong and should not be tolerated. However, people's points of view always differ. For example, some people may think that killing that happens during war is murder, while others will disagree, and that's where things get complicated. So, how are standards set for society? Can every act be covered under what ought to be?

Legal rights are those rights that are provided to us through things like the Constitution and include things like the right to bear arms or freely practice a chosen religion. These are rights that are man-made and are a set of laws that people in a specific society must follow.

Rights that are innate, that we believe every human should have, are called natural rights. These are rights given to us at birth that are universal and based on principles like expression, thought, beliefs, customs and even privacy. Some people believe that these rights are granted by a higher power, while others believe that these rights are simply an innate part of being a human. Let's see some examples of the differences between these two types of rights.

Under natural rights, one has a right to expression, yet under man-made law in the US, one cannot commit slander, or verbally defame someone's character by making false statements that can harm a person's reputation. In order to make sense of this, philosophers, like Locke and Kant, developed ethical theories to help us find the path to making right decisions.

Ethical Theories: In this section, we will explore several ethical theories. Following are some of them:

Deontology is about strict adherence to rules regardless of consequences. For example, people who believe that the death penalty should always be enforced even though some innocent people are executed might be described as having a deontological point of view.

The deontologist seems noble in his actions. But there is a negative side to this type of person. Suppose we meet a deontologist who believes that it his obligation to provide the financial stability for his family.

If this deontologist were to lose his job, he may no longer be able to provide for his family. Let's say his children are starving and need some food, and his wife tells him that if he does not rob a grocery store across the street, the children could die. Our deontologist would never rob that grocery store because he knows it's illegal. It's against the rules to rob a store, and the consequence of his children starving is less important to him than the rules.

Consequentialism is another ethical school of thought. Consequentialists believe that actions are defined as good or bad based on the consequence for their action. In other words, the end result justifies the means. A consequentialist may believe that the price of gasoline is too high and, thus, be a proponent of war on countries that control oil. So, if killing a few thousand soldiers is required in order to get cheaper oil, then the end justifies the means.

Some theorists believe **ethical relativism** is the right thing to do. This means what is morally right or wrong depends on the norms in one's culture. This means that there is no one universal moral code by which all people live.

This theory can be related to the issue of undocumented migrant farm workers in the United States. It has been common practice amongst some farmers to hire undocumented immigrants to harvest crops. This is done mostly because these workers are willing to work for very low wages and no benefits. The problem with this practice is that it affects competition amongst farmers that hire documented workers and pay a legal and fair wage.

Depending on your relative position on low wages and the immigration debate, you may find it ethically acceptable and fair for these farmers to pay undocumented workers at a lower-than-legal wage, or you may find it exploitative and morally reprehensible.

On the other hand, **moral absolutism** holds that the same standards apply in every situation regardless of culture or other factors. Let's say you meet a woman from Sweden who thinks it is morally wrong for the United States to provide no public healthcare for its citizens. Even though many Americans have value systems that do not emphasize public care programmes the way most Swedish people do, your new friend from Sweden believes that it is morally wrong for the US to have no public healthcare system. The cultural differences between these two countries do not make a difference to her in this case. She is seeing the situation through moral absolutism.

Sometimes, it comes down to a person's reputation. **Virtue ethics** says that it is not a person's actions that determines whether he is moral or not; it is his character that should be taken into consideration when making judgment. A person who generally treats people well will be less likely to be judged as immoral when committing an act against society than someone who habitually and deliberately hurts others.

Care ethics reminds us that people are relational beings and require care in relationships. Adherents to this theory believe that there is no set of standards that define what is right or wrong. It is more about taking another person's feelings into consideration when making moral decisions.

Assisted suicide may be an example of care ethics. Even if you believe that killing others is wrong, you might have a different point of view if the person being killed wants to die because they are suffering. This form of ethics is unlike the others as it is more psychological than calculated.

Each ethical principle relies on its own standard. This helps to explain why society cannot solely depend on moral code. Laws must be established as this ensures a true set of standards to which behaviour can be measured.

In sum, **ethics** involves a standard of what is right and wrong based on what people ought to do. It speaks to our obligation to society, what benefits society and what is fair. Ethical principles cannot replace law.

Natural rights are rights given to us at birth that are universal and should be granted to every human in every society, like expression, thought, beliefs, customs and even privacy. **Legal rights** are a set of laws that people in a specific society must follow.

CAUSES OF UNETHICAL BEHAVIOUR

Have you ever taken credit for something someone else did at work? For example, your boss stops by your office to tell you that your work on the marketing report was excellent, and he is rewarding you with a promotion. The problem is that most of the report was based on the hard work of your co-worker. Should you tell your boss that the co-worker really deserves the promotion? What makes you confess to your boss?

Usually, the answer is your business ethics. Business ethics refers to the moral principles or values that generally govern the conduct of an individual or group.

Ethical behaviour is acting in ways that are consistent with how the business world views moral principles and values. Business ethics determine employees' everyday conduct. Let's take a look at some of the factors that affect your ethical behaviour in the workplace. How would you answer when faced with an ethical dilemma?

Individual Factors

Many individual factors affect a person's ethical behaviour at work, such as knowledge, values, personal goals, morals and personality. The more information that you have about a subject, the better chance you will make an informed, ethical decision.

For example, what if you had to decide whether to approve building a new company store?

Values

Values are an individual's judgment or standard of behaviour. They are another individual factor that affect ethical behaviour. To some people, acting in an improper way is just a part of doing business. Would you feel that it is ethical to make up lies about your competitor just to win a contract? Some people's standard of behaviour will feel that lying for a business financial win is not unethical.

Morals

Morals are another individual characteristic that can affect an individual's ethics. Morals are the rules people develop as a result of cultural norms and values and are, what employees learn from their childhood, culture, education, religion, etc. They are usually described as good or bad behaviour. Would you have good morals if you pushed a product on a customer that you knew was not going to help solve a problem?

Many ethical work situations will also be affected by a person's goals. Which characteristics do you feel are worthy to aspire to? Is financial gain ranked ahead of good character or integrity? If your personal goals are about acquiring wealth no matter what the consequence, then you might act unethical in the future.

Lastly, an employee's personality plays an important factor in determining ethical behaviour. Do you enjoy risk or do you prefer the safe route? Individuals who prefer to take risks tend to have a higher chance of unethical conduct at work. For example, if you are willing to risk dumping chemicals into a nearby water supply to launch a profitable drug, then your riskiness could end up creating health issues in local citizens for the sake of financial gain.

Social Factors

Cultural norms, the Internet and friends and family are three social factors that can affect ethical behaviour. Different cultures have norms that vary from place to place in the business world. For example, you might have to face a request for a bribe in order to conduct business in certain countries in South America. This might be unethical to you but considered an acceptable norm in their workplace.

Friends, family and co-workers also play an important role in your ethical decision-making. If you witness your father bringing home business supplies every month from work, would you believe it is ethical to steal staplers, envelopes, etc. from your place of business? Lastly, the Internet has a tremendous impact on a worker's ethical behaviour. Would you think it is appropriate to post proprietary work information on your social media accounts? How about using work time to shop on the Internet? Many companies have implemented monitoring programmes to watch how their employees utilize the Internet.

Situational Opportunities

The third major factor that can influence ethical behaviour in the workplace are situational opportunities. These opportunities can provide an unethical employee with the freedom of choice that can lead to bad decisions. Most companies establish policies and procedures to provide ethical guidelines to employees. These are known as ethical codes and can establish checks and balances to support ethical behaviour.

For example, have you ever noticed that when you use a company credit card, your employer requires detailed information about the purchase, including description, amount, and an original receipt? This is to ensure proper use of the spending of company money. Some companies have strict policies stating no personal phone calls on company cell phones. This can be easily monitored by auditing an employee's bill.

ETHICAL ABUSES

The ethical behaviour of many professionals is regulated by codes of conduct. These codes tend to vary from one industry to another. Many of the regulations, though adjusted for each industry, are similar, however. Common ethics abuses include mishandling of client funds, conflict of interest, and lapsed licensing.

Improper or fraudulent billing are ethical abuses that can involve charging customers for services they did not receive. This happens in the medical industry, since the party who receives the bill is often not the party who received the services. The commonness of these ethical violations has led many insurance companies to issue a list of services to patients, encouraging them to report discrepancies. This ethical abuse is observed against hospitals which provide cashless facility under health/medical policies.

There are several ways a professional can commit ethical violations regarding the handling of client funds. A prime example is not placing client funds into an escrow account, which is an account where monies such as deposits are often kept. Managing such accounts is often required for attorneys and real estate agencies. If they fail to do so and place client monies into personal or business accounts, they are generally in violation.

Many professionals are required to renew or update their licenses and certifications. This often requires that courses be taken or fees be paid. For various reasons, many professionals do not renew their documents in time. Since many clients do not check these things, these ethical abuses often go unnoticed if a regulatory body does not discover them.

Crossing sexual boundaries are ethical abuses that differ from sexual harassment or sexual abuse. In these cases, both parties may be willing participants. However, something about the sexual relationship is inappropriate due to the professional's position. This can be found in a mental health setting when a psychiatrist engages in a sexual relationship with a client he knows to be emotionally or sexually vulnerable.

Conflict of interest usually involves a professional who violates her client's trust or places him at risk of harm because of her dealings with another individual. These situations may arise with attorneys or consultants. In these instances, they may provide information or engage in activities with opposing parties that jeopardize their clients. A good example is a criminal defense lawyer who dates his client's prosecutor.

Improper handling of documentation can also be found in numerous industries. These include the financial, health and legal industries. Many of the documents and files these professionals deal with contain sensitive and confidential information. When those items are carelessly handled or not secured according to standards, people's privacy, finances, and safety can be jeopardized.

These are some examples of ethical abuses.

WORK ETHICS

Workplace ethics refers to the application of values to decisions concerning employees in the organization. It involves right and wrong actions that directly influence the workplace. As it relates to ethical issues relating to hiring, promotion, wages, etc. of the human resources of an organization, it may be called internal ethics. Workplace ethics is an extension of the personal standards of the people who comprises the workplace. Several moral and ethical issues are involved in employer-employee relations. Ethics in the workplace require abolition of all kinds of discrimination and explanation.

An organization is basically a group of human beings. Therefore, people working in it should have a common understanding of what is right and wrong. They should feel free to discuss ethical issues. The primary responsibility for creating such an environment lies with the employer.

Your employees face ethical dilemmas every day in the workplace. They might be tempted to leave work early, take credit for the work of others or lie to a potential client to get him to sign the insurance policy, order the service or purchase the product that they are selling. The key to fostering strong business ethics at your company is to create an ethics policy that clearly spells out what is acceptable and unacceptable behaviour.

Cheating the Company

A solid ethics policy should clearly outline the procedure employees should follow if they need to take time off, leave early or start late. If you don't spell out these procedures, employees might be tempted to handle these matters on their own. They might claim to be meeting a client at the end of the workday when instead they are leaving early to catch cricket match on TV. They might claim to be at a workshop for the first half of the day when instead they are sneaking in some extra sleep. Make sure your ethics policy contains a provision telling your employees how they can request time off even for personal matters. Open communication is a far better alternative than the sneaking around required when employees try to cloak the reasons for their late starts or absences.

Working with Clients

Your ethics policy also should make it clear that your workers must treat clients and customers fairly and honestly. This means prohibiting employees from lying to potential clients or providing them with misleading information. Employees shouldn't hide the true price of a service, policy or product in an effort to trick customers into signing up. They also shouldn't promise more than their service or product can deliver. Employees should never bully or harass potential clients. Your ethics policy should state how often your workers can contact potential customers, at what times of the day and what exactly they can and cannot say during their conversations.

Abusive Behaviour

Any effective ethics policy forbids abusive behaviour in your workplace. This kind of behaviour can take many forms. Employees might engage in sexual harassment, bully other workers, tell inappropriate or offensive jokes, display pornography on their computer screens or steal from co-workers or the company. Your ethics policy must explicitly state that all such actions are forbidden at work. It also needs to spell out the punishments or repercussions of such actions.

Undue Credit

Some employees might try to rise in your company by taking credit for work that others employees actually performed. This can have a negative impact on morale if it goes unquestioned. Make sure your ethics policy prohibits this behaviour, too. Take seriously employee complaints that their fellow workers are stealing their ideas or taking credit for the reports, proposals or sales they complete.

Harassment

Harassment means intimidating and tormenting an individual or group of persons through constant interference. All acts and conducts that create a hostile or offensive working environment, amount to harassment. Such an environment unreasonably interferes with an individual's freedom and work performance.

Sexual harassment is usually committed by one employee against another. But the employer bears both legal and ethical obligations to prevent harassment. The following programmes may be undertaken to prevent cases of sexual harassment:

- Sexual harassment policy
- Communicating the policy
- Establishing procedures
- Taking appropriate actions

Whatever your hands find to do, do it with all your heart, with all your might and with all your strength! In short, put every emotion you have into it! If you find yourself doing something you're not emotionally attached to, it is probably time to make a change. You can only find fulfilment in doing what you love.

Ethical behaviour at the workplace can offer the following benefits:

(i) Better image and reputation of the enterprise in the industry and the community

(ii) Ability to attract and retain talented people

(iii) Reduced risk and employees making unethical decisions

(iv) Competitive advantage in the marketplace

(v) Lesser costs and hassles of legal action

An adequate internal forum will avoid the need for employees to report violations of ethical norms to outside regulatory agencies.

The main factors influencing the level of workplace ethics are as follows:

(i) The individual: The moral standards and values of a person exercise a significant impact on ethics in the workplace. An individual's values are tested frequently in the job situations. His decisions and actions reflect the understanding of his ethical responsibility as an employee.

(ii) Colleagues: Peers, the boss and subordinates exert influence on workplace ethics. The authority of the boss and the examples set by colleagues exercise control on the workplace decisions and actions of the individual.

(iii) Corporate culture: Company policies and codes are an important influence on workplace ethics. When a company's culture provides no direction regarding ethical conduct, confusion and conflict take place creating opportunity for unethical behaviour.

An individual has to face several ethical issues in the workplace. Some of these issues are given below:

(i) In relation to other employees

- (a) discrimination
- (b) harassment

(ii) In relation to customers

- (a) compromising with product safety
- (b) unfair pricing
- (c) deceptive advertising

(iii) In relation to suppliers
  (a) bribery
  (b) accepting gifts and favours
  (c) discrimination
  (d) dishonest contracts
(iv) In relation to company resources
  (a) use of company resources for personal benefit
  (b) embezzlement
  (c) tax evasion
  (d) disclosing company secrets

In his relationships and responsibilities at the workplace, an individual has to make choices between alternatives.

Conflict of Interest

A conflict of interest exists when an individual has to make a choice between self-interests and the interest of his/her organization. Enron Corporation collapsed primarily due to conflict of interest.

Discrimination

One of the oldest unfair practices that exist all over the world is discriminating. It has been prevalent both in developing and developed countries. Discrimination means differentiating among people not on the basis of individual merit but on the basis of prejudice or some other wrongful and illicit ground. Job discrimination or discrimination in employment refers to making adverse decisions against employees who belong to a certain class due to prejudice towards members of that class.

CODE OF CONDUCT

A statement and description of required behaviours, responsibilities, and actions expected of employees of an organization or of members of a professional body. A code of conduct usually focuses on ethical and socially responsible issues and applies to individuals, providing guidance on how to act in cases of doubt or confusion. These are a set of rules to guide behaviour and decisions; a way of behaving – a set of unwritten rules according to which people in a particular group, class, or situation are supposed to behave.

To be recognized as an ethical organization, corporate code should be designed in such a way that it guides the employees to behave in an ethical manner. The corporate code of conduct spells out what is to be done and what should not be done by the business unit. Corporate code of conduct is generally a more blanket statement of values and beliefs that defines the organization or group.

A corporate code incorporates a company's values. Thus, it is necessary for every organization to develop a corporate code. The development of a corporate code involves the identification of the key behaviour that maximizes long-term value, reviewing the codes, communicating the codes to employees, and finally updating the codes according to the laws and regulations. Once the code is developed, it has to be implemented in the organization.

Every organization whether large or small, has its own corporate code. Corporate codes reflect the purpose of the company and guide the companies to behave in an ethical manner. A corporate code refers to those policy statements that lay down the company's ethical standards. They are designed to govern the conduct of the employees. Corporate code enhances clarity of strategy, better decision-making, clearer communication and ease of delegation and inspires to have a greater commitment and loyalty for the organization.

Corporate codes are voluntary to organizations and enhance the freedom to address any issue such as employee's safety and health, worker's rights, etc. Implementation of the corporate code is dependent upon the company concerned. The CEO, Board of Directors, legal department, consultants and top management formulate the corporate code. In some organizations, employee representatives and selected employees may be involved in the formulation of the corporate code.

The success of a code of conduct depends on its credibility. These codes are considered to be credible when their existence and meaning is widely known to various groups such as contractors, workers, and the Government. To be credible and successful, these codes must be transparent, easy to enforce and monitor.

A code can be made transparent by disseminating and by imparting training regarding its provisions. Monitoring implies the validation of the code. This can be internal or external. Internal monitoring involves monitoring by setting a committee, ombudsman, regular reporting obligation, regular field visits or hotlines. External monitoring involves monitoring by an outside auditor, consultant, etc.

Why Code of Conduct?

As conducting business on ethical lines becomes increasingly popular, most of the business organizations are opting to implement a code of ethics:

- To define the framework of acceptable behaviour;
- To follow high standards of practice;
- To create benchmarks for self-evaluation;
- To enhance sense of community;
- To create transparency in business activities;
- To foster higher standards of business ethics; and
- To comply with Government laws and norms.

More and more businesses are developing a code of conduct so that customers can expect the minimum standards and predict corporate behaviour.

Unlike labour law, corporate codes of conduct do not have any authorized definition. The concept "corporate code of conduct" refers to companies' policy statements that define ethical standards for their conduct. There is a great variance in the ways these statements are drafted.

Corporate codes of conduct are completely voluntary. They can take a number of formats and address any issue — workplace issues and workers' rights being just is one possible category. Also, their implementation depends totally on the company concerned.

It is important that businesses conduct themselves in a legal and ethical manner. Code of conduct is related to business ethics and standards.

A code of conduct is a set of organizational rules or standards regarding organizational values, beliefs, ethics as well as matters of legal compliance that govern the conduct of the organization and its members. Organizational members are responsible for adhering to the code of conduct and will be held accountable for failure to do so. Most large businesses will have a code of conduct, which are often developed in response to legislation regulating business activities and behaviour or some sort of ethical scandal.

Types of Business Codes

You can actually break business ethical codes into three broad categories that are based upon the approach each takes in maintaining ethical and legal compliance. Let's take a short look at each.

- Codes of conduct typically prohibit behaviour and inform employees what is expected of them. Codes of conduct often outline penalties for failure to comply with the code. Common topics include conflicts of interest, political contributions, and acceptance of gifts.
- Codes of practice attempt to explain and illustrate the values and principles of the business. Instead of providing strict rules to follow, codes of practice educate employees on how 'things are done' in the business. These codes attempt to empower the employee by making her an ethical decision-maker.
- Codes of ethics codify the values and principles of the company and define the responsibilities, duties and obligations organizational members have to the organization and its stakeholders.

What's in Them?

While the content of codes will vary from organization to organization, many will address common topics, including:

- Conflicts of interests
- Confidential information
- Employment discrimination
- Use of the organization's property
- Financial reporting and accounting
- Health and safety issues
- Political contributions and campaigning in the office
- Legal compliance issues relevant to the organization

Examples: While many businesses have developed customized codes of conduct, some international organizations have developed international codes of conduct. Some examples include:

- International Chamber of Commerce
- Organization for Economic Cooperation and Development
- International Labor Organization
- United Nations Global Compact

Professional organizations also have developed codes of conduct that govern members of their professions. In fact, a professional's failure to comply with these codes can sometimes result in the professional being kicked out of the profession, such as a disbarred lawyer. Examples of professions that have developed professional codes of conduct include:

- Doctors – Hippocratic Oath
- Lawyers – Rules of Professional Conduct
- Engineers – National Society for Professional Engineers Code of Ethics for Engineers
- Nurses – American Nurses Association Code of Ethics
- CPAs – AICPA Code of Professional Conduct

PUBLIC GOOD

Public goods are any outcome that is open to all. Such an outcome is sharable; it is said to be non-rivalrous and non-excludable. It is hard to personally own and exchange public goods even though they can be enjoyed. A traffic light is a public good. One person can benefit in safely crossing a street and so can everyone else who passes by. But none of them owns the pole and light. Usually the government does. Non-rivalry means that consumption of the good by one individual does not reduce availability of the good for consumption by others. Non-excludability means that no one can be effectively excluded from using the good. Breathing air does not significantly reduce the amount of air available to others, and people cannot be effectively excluded from using the air. This makes air a public good, *albeit* one that is economically trivial, since air is a free good.

A standard list of public goods would include: peace, rule of law, a system of property rights and enforcement of contracts, communications and transportation systems, including the internet, the Linux community of software, beauty, knowledge and light houses.

Paul A. Samuelson is usually credited as the first economist to develop the theory of public goods. In his classic 1954 paper, 'The Pure Theory of Public Expenditure', he defined a public good, or as he called it in the paper as "collective consumption good", as follows: ...[goods] which all enjoy in common in the sense that each individual's consumption of such a good leads to no subtractions from any other individual's consumption of that good...

In the real world, there may be no such thing as an absolutely non-rivalled and non-excludable good; but economists think that some goods approximate the concept closely enough for the analysis to be economically useful.

One of the most basic of public goods is a state where individuals can enjoy their liberties, including use of property and the pursuit of happiness. This public good is protected by the rule that one person's freedom stops where it impinges on the equal freedom of others. Drawing the appropriate line between private right and limitations on that right to protect the rights of others is a messy process.

Where does my freedom to smoke end so that your liberty not to inhale second-hand smoke can be vindicated? Adam Smith in his lectures on jurisprudence called this intersection of private and public goods the problem of "police".

The production of public goods can also result in positive externalities which are not remunerated. If private organizations don't reap all the benefits of a public good which they have produced, their incentives to produce it voluntarily might be insufficient. Consumers can take advantage of such positive externalities or public goods without contributing sufficiently to their creation. This is called the free rider problem, or occasionally the "easy rider problem".

In the classic theory of the private firm, the business enterprise need not concern itself with public goods. It is to define its success or failure only with respect to the private goods or services it sells. Under this theory, as advocated with skill and passion by Milton Friedman and the Chicago School of economic thinking, if there are negative externalities spawned by the private sector creating a public concern, then it is up to government to step in and provide new, additional public goods in the form of regulation of private activity for the common good.

Thus, even in a theoretical world of purely private goods, there remains a problem along the border where something "public" arises to change the character of the private good into something of greater communal concern. The border must not only be defined it must be defended on both sides. The private goods side seeks to push the border farther away from its core autonomy and the public goods side seeks to prevent harm from crossing the border and to encourage positive externalities to be produced and shipped out "abroad" for public consumption. Watching over the border and adjusting disputes between the two sides is the function of CSR.

But outputs cannot so easily be allocated to just two categories of private and public. Some services that produce a public good, education for example, can be well delivered by private enterprise without government direction or supervision.

It may make more sense to think of a continuum of goods with completely private goods at one extreme and purely public goods at the other extreme. Next to fully private goods would come quasi-private goods and then a set of quasi-public goods before we get to purely public goods.

CHECK YOUR UNDERSTANDING

1. What is ethics? Explain the nature of ethics.
2. What are the characteristics of ethics?
3. Elucidate the causes of unethical behaviour. Give examples.
4. What is meant by ethical abuse? Give two examples for ethical abuse.
5. Explain work ethics with real-life examples.
6. What is code of conduct and list out the utility of code of conduct?
7. Write a brief note on public good. Give suitable examples.

REFERENCES

1. Riya Rupani: Business Ethics and Corporate Governance, Himalaya Publishing House, Mumbai.
2. Bhat, Govinda K. Dr. and Sumitha Ayodhya: Business Ethics and Corporate Social Responsibility, Himalaya Publishing House, Mumbai.
3. The Institute of Chartered Financial Analysts of India: Business Ethics and Corporate Governance, ICFAI Centre for Management Research, Hyderabad 500034.
4. Gupta, C.B.: Business Ethics and Communication, Sultan Chand & Sons, New Delhi, http://www.cauxroundtable.org

Chapter 3

Ethics Theory and Beyond

This Chapter deals with:

- Management of Ethics
- Ethics Analysis (Hosmer Model)
- Ethical Dilemma
- Ethics Practice
- Ethics for Managers
- Code of Ethics
- Ethics – Competitiveness, Organizational Size and Profitability
- Business and Ethical/Environmental Issues in India
- Case Studies

INTRODUCTION

Ethics programme is aimed at creation and maintaining a "do-it-right" climate. It ensures that employees' concerns, questions, and complaints are being heard and dealt with satisfactorily throughout the corporation.

This chapter deals with ethical issues like ethical dilemma, ethical practices, requirement of ethics for managers. It also inquires, the relationship of ethics with factors like competitiveness, organization size and profitability of the organization.

Organizations with code of ethics may define ethical behaviour, which is in accordance with their code. If the code is not developed through prolonged and extensive discussion, then it is unlikely to reflect the ethical views of the members of the organization. The development of a good code generally involves discussion among the members. Such discussion enables members to come to some sort of agreement about the basic values of business and means for solving the ethical dilemmas faced by the business.

MANAGEMENT OF ETHICS

"Right", "proper" and "fair" are ethical terms. These terms express a judgment about our behaviour towards other people that is felt to be just. We believe that there are right and wrong ways to behave towards others, proper and improper actions, fair and unfair decisions. These beliefs are our moral standards of behaviour. They reflect our sense of obligation to other people, our sense that it is better to help rather than to harm other people.

Moral problems are truly managerial dilemmas. They represent a conflict between an organization's economic performance (measured by revenues, costs and profits) and its social performance (stated in terms of obligations to persons both within and outside the organization).

Origination having ethics programmes should see that, it must be managed. It involves handling the employees' concerns, providing critical education, maintaining programme visibility and integrating the programme into the organization.

Handling employees concern includes dealing employee's questions, their concerns and complaints, providing them with immediate access to corporate ethics offices by means of toll-free or hotline etc.

Providing ethics education ensures employees to do right things.

Maintaining programme visibility internally can be done through posters, articles in the corporate magazine, speeches by senior executives and company newsletter. Integrating the programme into the organization treats its employees fairly and takes their complaints seriously.

ETHICS ANALYSIS (HOSMER MODEL)

Ethics and stakeholders theory states that the primary purpose of any organization is to maximize the stakeholder value. This theory states, "paying attention to the needs and rights of all the stakeholders of a business is a useful way of developing ethically responsible behaviour by managers". The theory acknowledges the fact that every business deals with a variety of stakeholders and any decision taken by the managers and the Board of Directors would have an impact on all the stakeholders. The theory also states that companies have responsibilities and obligations that extend beyond interest and needs of the shareholders. The point is, to decide what kind of responsibility that a company possesses. In an attempt to answer, Hosmer proposed five managerial responsibilities namely, ethical, conceptual, technical, functional and operational. Ethical responsibilities include the distribution of benefits and allocation of costs in a manner that is considered right, proper and just by the stakeholders.

Manager's Decision Checklist Provided by Hosmer

1. What are the best economic alternatives?
2. What are the legal alternatives?
3. Does a given decision result in greater benefits than damages for the society as a whole, not just for our organization as part of that society?
4. Is the decision self-serving, or would we be willing to have everyone else take the same action when faced with the same circumstances?
5. We understand the need for social cooperation; will our decision increase or decrease the willingness of others to contribute?
6. We recognize the importance of personal freedom; will our decision increase or decrease the liberty of others to act?

7. Lastly, we know that the universe is large and infinite, while we are small and our lives are short; is our personal improvement that important, measured against the immensity of that other scale?

ETHICAL DILEMMA

The success or failure of a business depends upon the decisions taken by the management. In making decisions, a manager often has to choose between alternatives. Sometimes the choice is clear, there is a right answer and a wrong answer. However, in many cases, the choice is more difficult, and this situation results in ethical dilemma, where no matter which alternative one selects, one has to make some sort of compromise.

Ethical dilemmas, by their very nature, involve a range of actions and their corresponding consequences. The problems arise due to their involvement in value judgments, which by their nature are rarely clear-cut. To resolve an ethical dilemma, one has to prioritize values to the extent possible and violate the least number possible.

Both employers and employees of an organization face dilemmas at work. Take the case of an employee, who on joining an organization discovers that senior managers are submitting inflated travel bills. The new employee is encouraged to do likewise. The employee now has to make a choice. Should he obey his seniors and submit travel bills, or should he be scrupulously honest in claiming travel allowance and thereby perhaps expose the supervisors?

Following are the ethical dilemmas, frequently occurring at workplace. What would you do in each case?

- The customer wants a refund. You agree that a refund is called for, but company policy says, " no refund". If you go to your supervisor, the customer will be denied a refund. If you act on your own authority, and give the customer a refund, the customer will be satisfied, but you may get into trouble.

- Quality is supposed to take precedence over everything else. The job you are about to finish is 'acceptable' but you know that you could do a 'quality' job if you spend two more hours on it. If you take the extra time, you will miss your deadline.

The most common ethical dilemmas in business relate to:

- Power, trust and authority
- Secrecy, confidentiality and loyalty.

Every manager enjoys a certain degree of power and authority, which is conferred on him by his position in the organization. He is expected to show equal care and concern for all individuals while performing his duties. Some decision made by managers could often be biased. An individual who has the power to take decisions in an organization, should make sure his decisions are seen as being fair and impartial.

At times, an organization hides certain information relating to the business from its employees, creditors, suppliers or even customers. In certain situations, organizations need to reveal certain information. But the point is – who is entailed to know the information? In any profession, maintaining confidentiality is essential for building trust among clients.

Ethical dilemmas commonly arise in the workplace. Who is going to resolve these dilemmas? The employees or the managers.

A manager has to perform multiple roles to take different tasks in the organization to complete the task. Depending on the task, he has to ask as a spokesperson, a planner while drafting a policy, a leader while leading his team etc. They justify their behaviour in resolving the dilemma rationalization.

Employees can also be asked to help resolve ethical dilemmas. In many organizations, the absence of commonly held beliefs and values can give rise to ethical dilemmas. And in many other organizations, problems arise because the beliefs and values of the company may not been made public. As a result, employees have to determine for themselves, through their mistakes, what is 'acceptable' behaviour.

ETHICS PRACTICE

Ethical practice is not one-time exercise and is a walk of life both for individuals and businesses. If the owners of the business act ethically, there is no reason why a business will act unethically. In business, there are different functions where ethical practiccs are required and practiced.

You'll find lots of examples of business ethical decisions and dilemmas in areas such as:

- Advertising
- Personal selling
- Business contracts
- Pricing
- Dealing with suppliers

Let's take one of the above – suppliers.

A business cannot claim to be ethical firm if it ignores unethical practices by its suppliers, e.g.,

- Use of child labour and forced labour
- Production in sweatshops
- Violation of the basic rights of workers
- Ignoring health, safety and environmental standards

An ethical business has to be concerned with the behaviour of all businesses that operate in the supply chain, i.e.,

- Suppliers
- Contractors
- Distributors
- Sales agents

Pressure for Businesses to Act Ethically

Businesses and industries increasingly find themselves facing external pressure to improve their ethical track record. An interesting feature of the rise of consumer activism online has increased scrutiny of business activities. Pressure groups are a good example of this. Pressure groups are external stakeholders. They:

- Tend to focus on activities and ethical practice of multinationals or industries with ethical issues
- Combine direct and indirect action that can damage the target business or industry

Direct consumer action is another way in which business ethics can be challenged. Consumers may take action against:

- Businesses they consider to be unethical in some ways (e.g. animal furs)
- Business acting irresponsibly
- Businesses that use business practices they find unacceptable

Consumer action can also be positive – supporting businesses with a strong ethical stance and record.

Is Ethical Behaviour Good or Bad for Business?

You might think the above question is an easy one for businesses to answer? Surely acting ethically makes good business sense? As with all issues in business studies, there are two sides to every argument: The advantages of ethical behaviour include:

- Higher revenues – demand from positive consumer support
- Improved brand and business awareness and recognition
- Better employee motivation and recruitment
- New sources of finance, e.g., from ethical investors

The disadvantages claimed for ethical business include:

- Higher costs, e.g., sourcing from fair trade suppliers rather than lowest price
- Higher overheads, e.g., training and communication of ethical policy
- A danger of building up false expectations

ETHICS FOR MANAGERS

Businesses are driven by profit motives. Managers should consider that ethics is not a hindrance and rather a driver of business. If managers of business accept this argument, entire organization becomes an ethical organization. Some of the ethical practices the managers need to concentrate are:

1. Truthfulness, kindness and respects for others
2. Not accepting and giving bribe for quicker results
3. Following the law of the land
4. Following best practices of safety in production
5. Conscious efforts to reduce environmental harm by setting necessary best processes, though it may involve costs
6. Payment of taxes and desist from avoidance of taxes by illegal means
7. Following the proper accounting systems and maintaining proper books of accounts
8. Following corporate governance
9. Orienting towards corporate social responsibility and doing some thing worthwhile to the society
10. Sharing the gains of business equitably among all the stakeholders of business
11. Treating the employees well and following best HR practices
12. Acting as a role model in ethical behaviour so that the subordinates draw clear signals. The General Managers and other managers will take right ethical decision if business managers live by example

All the employees look to managers for their ethical behaviour. Therefore, managers have important role to inculcate ethics in their organization in all walks of business right from production, advertising, marketing, servicing the product, pricing , accounting and sharing of gains.

CODE OF ETHICS

Many companies use the phrases 'ethical code' and 'code of conduct' interchangeably but it may be useful to make a distinction. A code of ethics will start by setting out the values that underpin the code and will describe a company's obligation to its stakeholders. The code is publicly available and addressed to anyone with an interest in the company's activities and the way it does business. It will include details of how the company plans to implement its values and vision as well as guidance to staff on ethical standards and how to achieve them. However, a code of conduct is generally addressed to and intended for employees alone. It usually sets out restrictions on behaviour, and will be far more compliance or rules focused than value or principle focused. Also this code is good for the Non-governmental Organization.

A code of ethics is a guide of principles designed to help professionals conduct business honestly and with integrity. A code of ethics document may outline the mission and values of the business or organization, how professionals are supposed to approach problems, the ethical principles based on the organization's core values and the standards to which the professional will be held.

Code of ethics are mainly values, which specify behaviour of its employees and these values are basis for creation of code of given institution. There are many positives in usage of codes:

1. Ethical code may help in relationship building between managers and employees that they can share the same principles and values.
2. Codes can help managers in situations when they are not sure how to act – when they do not know which decision is more accurate when dealing with ethical issue.
3. Code helps manager when he is speaking with partners from other companies.
4. Code helps both managers and employees to realize their duties and competence. It is a guide for both employees and managers.

ETHICS – COMPETITIVENESS, ORGANIZATIONAL SIZE AND PROFITABILITY

If there is a feeling that competitiveness and profitability get affected due to ethics based dealings; or ethics cannot be followed by big businesses, it is a myth. There are corporate examples which show that businesses can be run ethically and it helps achieve its business goals.

Business Ethics and Competitiveness

There is a general feeling that the competitiveness of the business is affected if business is run ethically. It is also believed that ethics is a hindrance for business. It is factually incorrect. The firms which follow the ethics are better respected and public confidence on such businesses increases and business improves in the long term. For example, Tata Group is known for running the businesses ethically. This has given an edge to all Tata products, right from its automobiles to edible oil products. The business enjoys the trust and patronage on account of following of ethics. Though, it may appear that the competitiveness of the business is affected by ethical following, in the long run it pays. Cases are not wanting where unethical businesses are thrown out or refused by the society. For example, the Sahara Group company's faced public wrath and even the judiciary was very harsh and strict to bring the culprits to their senses. Therefore, ethics does not negatively affect competitiveness, instead impacts positively.

Business Ethics and Organizational Size

For following the business ethics, the size of the business does not matter. Irrespective of the size, all businesses can follow the ethics if there is an organizational will. Tata Steel unit of Jamshedpur, is a massive establishment, but ethics is followed to such an extent that the entire town respects the ethical mindset shown by the promoters in testing times. The organizational culture of ethics has percolated to ordinary employee of the company.

Ethics is followed with rigour in all the group companies of Tata, which is one of the largest group of business in India. There are enough examples of fly-by-night companies which are unethical. Therefore, organizational size does not matter for following the business ethics. It is all the more important that larger businesses follow the ethics and it will compel other companies dealing with the large company to be ethical. When a large company follows ethics, the suppliers, dealers, financiers, regulators and even the Government is forced to follow the ethics while dealing with the company. Such is the formidable reputation which Tata Group has developed. The group stands out in not giving any bribe to the bureaucrats or the politicians for its legitimate rights to get commercial permissions. Such is the commitment the group has developed under its great founders. It is a mute question, how many such companies exist in India?

Business Ethics and Profits

Survival is the name of any business game. If a company wants to survive, it has to think about its profits. Most businesses operate on the principle that profit is not linked to ethical consideration. But there are instances, which nullify the above principle. For instance, Johnson & Johnson is often recognized as a company whose ethical behaviour is exemplary. The company clearly prioritize its responsibilities in its corporate credo: first to its customers, second to its employees, third to its management, fourth to the communities in which it operates, and fifth to its stockholders. "Business must make a sound profit" states the credo in describing fifth responsibility, but at Johnson & Johnson that concern comes after rest.

In 1982, the company decided to recall 31 million bottles of Tylenon from store shelves after eight people died from cyanide-laced capsules. This recall costed Johnson & Johnson $ 240 million and cut its profits by $ 5 billion or 50 per cent of its revenue. The tempering was not company's fault, but it decided to act even before, as it had complete information on what had happened. The product containers were redesigned and new tamper-proof packaging was introduced. Johnson & Johnson's immediate response not only saved the Tylenol brand but also won the applause of the customers.

The term 'profit' in business is appropriate, but 'only profit' is not acceptable any more. Today, every organization, whether big or small, has to justify its existence in the marketplace. It is felt that if company cannot generate profits, it has no right to exist in the marketplace. A firm that is not performing well is considered as liability and burden to the society, as it cannot discharge its responsibility to the community welfare to its employees, revenue to shareholders, and meet customer demands. Thus, profit today is recognized as a characteristic of the success of a business and a justification for its existence.

A sick or loss making company is bound to misuse scarce resources. Such a loss making company makes huge liabilities; upsets the business, promotes inefficiency and finally cannot discharge its social responsibility. Considering this situation, it may be unethical for a firm to make loss. Such firms cannot exist in the marketplace as they force their employees into economic insecurity.

BUSINESS AND ETHICAL/ENVIRONMENTAL ISSUES IN INDIA

Global Scenario

In today's global environment, environmental ethics have become a required practice for everyone around the world. Creating effective strategies for protecting the environment often brings ethical issues to the forefront. When people are confronted with the issues of how to get rid of hazardous waste, air or water pollution, ethics play a major role in the decision when there is an absence of laws to manage the issue.

Environmental ethics is the scientific study of various issues related to the rights of individual on the environment. It is the moral relationship of human being with the environment. The actions humans do while on this Earth can affect the rights of all the beings today and in the future. Knowing what is right and wrong can help protect future generations. One must know the standards to help conserve the Earth's resources and the consequences.

Environmental ethics is a moral theory that grants moral significance to entities beyond those that are human beings. This means that humans not only have rights but all living organisms as well. We must not forget we are not the only creature living and breathing on this Earth.

Now that we know how environmental ethics work. Let's take a look at some example situations. In the past few decades, a rapid growth in new technology has changed the way society works, communicates, interacts, and lives. Many of these innovations focus on the design, production, and use of electronic and electrical equipment ranging from computers to cellphones to digital cameras to smart appliances. The constant change for new more advanced technology makes current models outdated after only a few months or years. Once outdated, society throws away these items making them e-waste (electronic waste) or e-scrap (electronic scrap). This has become a problem for the waste management community. This electronic waste contains toxins like lead, mercury, and polychlorinated biphenyls, and components that possess great monetary value like gold, platinum and copper. Lead can damage both the central and peripheral nervous systems. Beryllium and cadmium can be carcinogenic. Arsenic used in circuits and conductors is poisonous and can damage the digestive tract. Mercury found in batteries can damage the central nervous and endocrine systems. Antimony also used in batteries is poisonous like arsenic. We don't want this waste to contaminate our water or soils. Companies that produce these constantly evolving technologies may have an environmental obligation. The chemicals they use to produce these innovations are obviously dangerous to our environment if they are not disposed correctly. Most of these companies do not advocate the promotion of correctly recycling these products. Instead environmental enthusiasts and waste companies are stuck with the responsibility of influencing society to do the right thing. The ethical question technology producing companies need to ask their self is do we have a responsibility of helping manage our products future waste? In a way, they should take responsibility for future product waste because it's simply their product that could affect our environment. Can they deal with the moral debt of allowing their product damage human bodies and our soils? On the other hand, waste management must take on whatever waste consumers dispose of and correctly manage this waste. That is their sole duty and should companies have to share this duty?

Another rising concern for the world is global warming. Wastes and chemicals used by nuclear power, electronic waste and chemical waste affect the ozone layer. Our air layer is polluted by wastes developed by production and consumption processes as a result of human activities and it endangers the life of humans and living beings on earth. Our air which has an indispensable place and importance for the continuity of life on earth is polluted with industrial wastes that affect the entirety of life. Greenhouse gases which cause the greenhouse effect (warming of the Earth) in the world are 36-70 per cent for water vapour, 9-26 per cent for carbon dioxide, 4-9 per cent for methane and 3-7 per cent for ozone. Some of greenhouse gases are created by themselves and some of them are produced by humans. The most important one of greenhouse gases which cause global warming is carbon dioxide (CO_2) and its ratio in total greenhouse gases is more than 80 per cent. CO_2 is often created as a result of burning of fossil-fuels. It can also be created from natural things like organic decay, forest fires, and volcanoes. CO_2 is the most recalcitrant of the greenhouse gases, since it does not decompose easily in the atmosphere.

Indian Scenario

Environmental ethics is a branch of applied ethics, which examines the moral basis of environmental responsibility. Environmental responsibilities have to be weighted against the responsibilities to stakeholders and societal benefits, as any damage caused to environment has an impact on society as well as on stakeholders.

Environmental issues such as toxic waste, contamination of groundwater, oil spills destroying the seashores, fossil fuels producing carbon dioxide resulting in greenhouse effect, usage of fluoro carbons that depletes the ozone layer etc. can be tackled by espousing environmental ethics. Thus, the goal of environmental ethics does not mainly revolve around the concern about the environment but it is concerned about the moral foundation of environmental responsibility, and the limit up to which this responsibility expands.

Environmental Issues

When there is no strong governing body for formulating and implementing on environmental policy and when there is lack of adequate environmental expertise, technology and resources for environment protection, environment degradation goes unchecked. Following paragraphs look at some of the environmental issued faced by India.

Rapid industrialization and urbanization have brought about economic development in India, but they also caused damage to the country's environment through deforestation, soil erosion, water pollution etc. The Government of India has adopted a comprehensive policy to protect public health, forests and wildlife. But the policy has an important limitation that no court can enforce it.

The Environmental Protection Act (1986) focused on reducing industrial pollution. The report stated that the estimated annual cost of environmental degradation in 4.5 per cent of GDP (average) A majority of the environmental issues that India faces are related to air pollution.

Air Pollution

According to the World Health Organization (WHO) environmental report, New Delhi is one of the top ten most polluted cities in the world. It was found that respiratory diseases caused due to air pollution in New Delhi are about 12 times the national average. Also premature deaths occurring each year due to air pollution is the highest in the country.

To curb vehicular emission, the Supreme Court of India has laid down two rules. All public vehicles that are 15 or more than 15 years old should be banned, and Public transport vehicles in New Delhi should switch over to Compressed Natural Gas (CNG) engines. But these regulatory reforms, which were aimed at minimizing air pollution problems, have failed due to lack of enforcement.

Energy Consumption and Carbon Emission

India is the second largest commercial energy consumer in non-OECD in East Asia. 60 per cent of its energy needs are met by commercial energy and non-conventional and renewable fuels meet 40 per cent of its energy needs.

In India, carbon emission has grown nine times over the past four decades. Its contribution to world carbon emission is expected to increase by 3.2 per cent (1996-2020). The country's reliance on low-quality coal with high carbon content is the primary reason for high carbon emission.

The problem of carbon emission can be solved by relying on technology that reduces the amount of coal consumed or use of better grade coal. Several programmes were initiated to improve the efficiency of coal usage. These programmes which were co-ordinated by Coal India Limited and were designated to ensure the conservation of coal resources during production, and improvement of end-use technologies.

Energy and Carbon Intensity

Carbon intensity levels are high in India, when compared to other Asian countries. The reason for this are the increase in industrial activity that has taken place due to economic expansion, and the absence of energy and conservation measures in most industrial areas. Indian economic policies such as high impact tariffs on high quality coal and subsidies on low-quality coal, have also contributed to carbon pollution intensity. Recently, the Indian government took initiatives to encourage the usage of higher quality coal. Coal tariffs have been reduced to 35 per cent and the use of the washed coal is mandatory in all power plants from 2001 onwards.

Environmental Management in India

Environmental practices in India have improved significantly in recent times. Being used to a fairly lax regulatory environment for a long period, many Indian companies had not taken environmental management seriously in the past. Now, regulations have become more stringent. Moreover, many companies are looking at environmental management as a means to improve their image and to cut costs. Many companies have quantifiable targets in areas such as emissions. Some companies stand out in their effort to upgrade environmental performance. Not surprisingly, quite a few of these companies are subsidiaries of global companies.

Bayer India believes that the benefits of successful environmental management programmes far outweigh the costs. The company has made substantial investments in incinerators and leased out 30 of its incineration capacity to other chemical firms. Philips India has taken its own steps to reduce pollution. So is Tata steel. Yet, the environmental management in India still has a long way to go. Consider the Uranium Corporation of India Ltd. (UCIL) mines in Jadugoda. Children in 15 adjoining villages have been affected by radiation, while many workers are suffering from serious ailments.

Many Indian companies look to ISO 14001 Certification as an end in itself. Most have not integrated environmental management into the corporate strategy. In many instances, "green initiatives" have been launched without a clear understanding of the potential benefits. In the worst cases, companies flout pollution laws and pay bribes to government inspectors when they visit their premises Quite clearly, Indian companies still have a long way to go in the area of environmental management. The cost they may have to incur in the event of mishap may turn out to be heavy!

India's Environment Policy

The Directive Principles of State Policy of the Indian Constitution commands the State to ensure protection and improvement of environment and to safeguard forest and wildlife. The Directive Principle of State Policy on Environment has been eloquently articulated in Article 48A of the Constitution, introduced by the 42nd Amendment in 1977. It reads thus: "The state shall endeavour to protect and improve the environment and to safeguard the forests and wildlife of the country". Likewise, Article 51(A)(g) lays down protection and improvement of environment as one of the fundamental duties of every citizen. This duty of citizens would mean that every citizen is duty-bound to protect and improve the natural environment of the country including forests, lakes and wildlife and to have compassion for all living creatures.

Laws Governing Environment

The Environment (Protection) Act, 1986 provides for the protection and improvement of environment and for matters connected therein. There were also other Acts enacted in India relating to environmental issues such as:

(i) Water (Prevention and Control of Pollution) Act, 1974

(ii) Air (Prevention and Control of Pollution) Act 1981 and

(iii) Factories' Amendment Act, 1987.

Environment pollution created by individuals or corporations amounts to public nuisance and therefore, this can be controlled through criminal law. Offensive smells, noise and air pollution are included under "nuisance". The public nuisance interferes with the quality of life of the society. Therefore, pollution originating from water, air and noise can be prevented by civil or criminal laws.

National Environmental Policy, 2004

This policy was released in August 2004. Environmentalists have welcomed it, because though it is more of a strategy paper than a policy pronouncement – it is still a welcome initiative, given the fact that a policy statement on environment and its effective implementation is long overdue, and that it is the dire need of the hour. The policy covers the following:

(i) conservation of life-supporting systems

(ii) forest and wildlife conservation

(iii) forest cover

(iv) biodiversity conservation

(v) concerns on fresh water resources

Ecological and environmental issues are ethical issues of business. Businesses have started recognizing this part of ethics and started responding favourably. Government has brought some laws though, they are not as well developed as in other developed countries.

CASE STUDIES

Case Study 1

Bio-fuel Policy and Potential in India

Due to increased energy demand, India must import energy to meet current demand. There is potential for bio-fuels to leverage indigenous sources of inputs, potentially increasing income and opportunities in rural areas. Yet the development of a bio-fuel sector could increase staple food prices and increase food insecurity for poor consumers.

Currently, bio-fuel production is minimal, accounting for only one per cent of global production. Supporting a future bio-energy sector will likely require policy support (such as stimulus packages), community and local interest, technological breakthroughs, and cost-effective feedstock production.

Why is India Important in This Conversation of Bio-fuels?

Bio-fuels are potentially important to India because of the significant number of lives they could impact and the economic changes they could cause. India is currently the second most populous nation in the world with a growing population of over 1.147 billion people. As of August 2008, the Indian government and the World Bank both estimated that 26 per cent of India's population was classified as poor despite efforts made to alleviate the problem. However, there are possibilities to ameliorate poverty through economic growth. According to the International Monetary Fund, the Indian economy is growing at over 7 per cent a year, which means there are opportunities to invest in new industries such as bio-fuels that could help resolve some of India's economic problems.

As the fifth largest energy consumer in the world, India additionally provides a good market for bio-fuels. 70 per cent of its crude oil is imported from around the world and experts anticipate that over 94 per cent of its crude oil will be purchased from abroad by 2030 if energy trends continue on their current trajectory. Bio-fuels offer potential opportunities to decrease the nation's dependence on foreign energy imports.

In India, bio-fuels are an alternative energy option due to the availability of feedstock crops. Since the sugar industry is one of India's largest industries, sugarcane and its processing byproduct are available for bio-ethanol production. Other feedstocks such as oil-seeds for bio-diesel are not yet widely available, but it is expected that trees such as *jatropha curcas* that produce these seeds will thrive in India's climate and environment.

What are Bio-fuel Options in India?

The term bio-fuels refers to several different types of fuels, including bio-ethanol and bio-diesel, which are both viable options in India. Bio-ethanol is the most common form of bio-fuel. It it likely that India would use molasses, a by-product of its sugar processing industry, to drive ethanol production.

On the other hand, there are major impediments to large-scale production and use of bio-ethanol in India including price competitiveness and production limitations. The price of bio-ethanol must be competitive with oil or other current energy sources in order to be successful. However, current production technologies force bio-fuel prices higher than those of traditional fuels. One way to lower prices is to couple India's sugar production with its bio-ethanol production so that the sugar industry absorbs some of the costs. However, it is likely that additional costs from bio-fuel production would cause the price of sugar products to rise for the general population. Additionally, bio-ethanol production from molasses might be hindered by the fact that the sugar industry is volatile as a result of its dependence on monsoons. More specifically, when monsoons are weak, less sugarcane grows and therefore, less molasses is available for bio-ethanol production. This effect was apparent in 2003 and 2004 when monsoons were more subdued than normal and, as a result, both sugar production and bio-ethanol production decreased dramatically.

Bio-diesel from oilseed plants are also an option for India's bio-fuel industry. Recently, Indian scientists, economists and politicians have become increasingly interested in jatropha, a plant that grows in arid or semi-arid tropical regions, and produces seeds containing anywhere between 21 per cent to 48 per cent oil. It is speculated that jatropha could be the answer to the food-versus-fuel debate because it grows on marginal land or around crops as a protective barriers without competing with them for natural resources. Moreover humans, and animals for that matter, do not normally eat jatropha, and thus there is little concern that jatropha will be diverted from food markets to fuel the energy industry.

There remain numerous questions about the feasibility of commercial jatropha production, because the concept to use the crop for bio-diesel is relatively new. For example, how well could it be grown for commercial production and how efficient can the conversion from oilseed to bio-diesel be? However, at a glance, jatropha seems like a potentially viable option to research for India's bio-fuel industry. Initial studies show that the oil from jatropha might support a good fuel economy because its production is economically competitive with diesel when fuel prices are high. In 2006, jatropha production was $ 0.47/liter while oil production was $ 0.46/liter.

Debate: Food vs. Fuel

Over the past few years, bio-fuel critics have argued that investments in bio-fuels will decrease food security in developing nations where there are already many people who cannot afford to buy food at current prices. It is expected that if grains and other staple foods are diverted from food markets into energy markets to produce bio-fuels, food prices will rise. As a result, basic sustenance will be less accessible to the poor around the world.

India is particularly vulnerable to food security issues. As of 2008, the United Nations Development Programme estimated that over 27 per cent of Indians live below the poverty line and lack access to enough calories per day to sustain a healthy lifestyle. As recently as 2006, India imported 2.2 million tonnes of wheat in order to ensure food availability. If more food is siphoned off from the food markets into the energy market to grow the bio-fuel industry, it is likely that the food-versus-fuel conflict will come into play.

Sugarcane and edible vegetable oils such as palm oil are two of the most common feedstocks for bio-fuel production around the world. However, there are concerns that India must steer clear of these two feedstock sources in order to avoid serious problems of food insecurity. India is already the largest consumer of the sugar in the world. If sugar were then additionally diverted to the bio-fuel industry, the food industry would be less able to meet its demand. UN researchers suggest that sorghum and tropical sugar beets would be better suited to drive India's bio-ethanol production. Similarly, India's demand for vegetable oil already outstrips its supply. However, non-edible oils could be used instead to produce bio-diesel.

Pro-bio-fuels experts claim that the impacts of bio-fuels can be mitigated through two major types of technological innovation. First, nations can focus on cellulosic bio-fuel technologies that use byproducts or waste products of food and other crops to create bio-fuels. Technologies necessary for this option to be feasible are just starting to become available but are relatively expensive. Similarly, investments in existing technologies that increase agricultural productivity could soften the impact of bio-fuels especially when coupled with technologies for cellulosic bio-fuel production. The choice does not necessarily need to be between food and fuel. However, the elimination of this conflict is highly dependent on India's willingness to invest in new technologies.

Debate: How Will Bio-fuels Impact Poor and Small Farmers in India?

The bio-fuel industry could have significant positive impacts on the health, education, and productivity of the rural poor population in India. Some anticipate that the bio-fuel industry will create new jobs for the poorest communities in India because bio-fuel production requires mostly unskilled labour, which is widely available in rural areas. Although many people worry that bio-fuels decrease food security, others counter that the opposite is true. Their argument is that food security is determined by one's ability to purchase food at the market price rather than by the abundance or shortage of food. If higher incomes result from increased employment, the rural poor will have more access to food even if prices rise. Furthermore, bio-fuel production has the potential to increase access of rural communities to cleaner, more reliable energy.

Although bio-fuel production has the potential to benefit India's rural poor, there is also the possibility of causing harm. If land is transferred from its current use for bio-fuel production, the poor will benefit from employment but may risk losing fodder for their livestock or materials for their houses and other structures. The Indian government cited that there were over 30 million hectares of wasteland available for jatropha production around the nation. However, a lot of this wasteland is also considered Common Property Resources (CPR), land that is collectively owned by rural villages and communities. This land is generally a source of food, fuel, fodder, timber, and thatching for the poorest in India. One study reports that 12-25 per cent of poor household incomes depend on CPR.

The well-being of the urban poor could be particularly endangered by the bio-fuels, in contrast with the rural poor who may have some opportunities to benefit. Although the urban poor do not risk losing their land to bio-fuel production, they don't gain employment opportunities or income increases from an expanded bio-fuel industry either. If India produces bio-fuels from food commodities on a large-scale or if other countries around the world decide to do so, global food prices will likely rise. The rural poor may be less affected by increased food prices as a result of their ability to produce their own food and live outside the global food market or due to their increased income as a result of bio-fuel production in rural areas. The urban poor have more at stake because their food security is more tightly linked to fluctuations in the global food market and because they are unlikely to reap any benefits or additional income from the bio-fuels industry.

There are also numerous questions concerning exactly who will benefit from the bio-fuel industry — small farmers or large corporations? As a result of the fact that so little is known about jatropha, small farmers are unlikely to risk planting jatropha, which will not reap any profits for 2 to 3 years, if at all. They are more likely to plant more conventional crops such as sugarcane, which can better ensure benefits but potentially endanger the food security of the entire poor population. For these reasons, larger companies might become the larger stakeholders in the bio-fuel industry, which could lead to greater losses but also greater gains. The question seems to be, whether bio-fuels widen or narrow the inequality gap?

Jatropha: Myth of Miracle

Some have hailed jatropha as the answer to India's energy conundrum. According to many sources, jatropha has long been used as a small-scale energy source. In Central America, where it originated, people often use the plant to create lamp oil. Proponents expect this small shrub-like plant to fuel the bio-fuels industry, supporting energy security and independence of the future. However, how much is actually known about this plant, and why are politicians and scientists alike considering it to be the "Holy Grail" of bio-fuel feedstocks.

Jatropha has numerous advantages over other feedstocks, which supports the notion that jatropha could be used as the primary feedstock for Indian bio-diesel. The plant species grows on wastelands with minimal water or nutrients, and has a relatively high oil yield per plant. According to estimates, one hectare of jatropha could yield about 1,892 liters of oil. Additionally, the plants produce seeds for a predicted 30 years. Jatropha contributes negligibly to the "Fuel vs. Food" debate because it is not edible for humans or other animals. Thus, growing jatropha for bio-fuel production neither pulls away nutrients from the food market nor requires valuable croplands due to its preference for arid soils.

Although jatropha comes with a host of positive attributes, it is important to keep in mind that decision-makers lack crucial information about jatropha, which is still essentially a wild plant. Questions still remain about how much water the plant requires in its first years of growth and whether plant density changes its growth potential. Since jatropha has never been fully domesticated it is more difficult to predict its yield year after year. Additionally, it still remains to be seen whether or not jatropha will actually the poor. Experimental results indicating low yields and financial returns have shed doubts on the pro-poor jatropha miracle. As a result, it is necessary to study the plant in depth in order to better understand its optimal growing environment and growth potential. Experts are, therefore, hesitant to recommend heavy investment in jatropha for commercial use before the plant is fully domesticated. Different jatropha varieties need to be explored in the future before it is planted and harvested like a conventional crop. However, in the mean time, jatropha can be used as a good fallow crop because it stops ground erosion and increases water storage in the soil.

The Policy Environment

Much support for Indian bio-fuels has come directly from the Indian national government. Its pro-bio-fuels policy agenda emphasizes an optimistic outlook of bio-fuels, indicating that these alternative fuels will bring greater energy security and independence to the nation. The development of a domestic bio-fuel market is anticipated to improve lives of the poor by creating more rural employment opportunities. Improved rural employment rates have the potential to have cascading effects that will contribute to the overall improvement of the health and well-being of the population. Lastly, the government hopes bio-fuels will be more environmentally friendly than other current energy sources by decreasing air pollution and possibly greenhouse gas emissions.

The government started moving its agenda on bio-fuels in 2003 with the introduction of the National Mission on Bio-fuels and the Ethanol Blending Programme (EBP). Under the National Mission, jatropha would be planted on 500,000 hectares of government land, and later expanded onto more land.

Simultaneously, the government hoped to begin privatizing the bio-diesel industry to become completely separate from the government by 2012. However, these plans did not come to fruition as a result of limited financial and policy support. EBP also encountered significant barriers. The programme mandated that oil companies produce fuel with 5 per cent ethanol in certain regions of the nation. The programme almost immediately grinded to a halt because there wasn't enough ethanol to meet this mandate between 2003 and 2004. Interestingly, the National Mission on Bio-fuels and EBP demonstrated to private investors that the Indian government is serious about testing the feasibility of bio-fuels. Numerous sources report that jatropha planting and other bio-fuel development has started despite unsuccessful government programmes.

In September 2008, the Indian government announced the National Bio-fuels Policy. The policy aims to blend conventional fuels with 20 per cent bio-ethanol or bio-diesel by 2017. The government recommends that bio-diesel be produced only from non-edible oilseeds, preferably those grown on marginal lands so as to minimize the food-versus-fuel debate. Emphasis is placed on developing the domestic growth and production of non-edible feedstocks and their resulting oils by creating a Minimum Support Price and Minimum Purchase Price, as well as by removing all taxes and duties levied on domestic bio-fuels. Finally, the National Policy calls for the creation of a Bio-fuel Steering Committee, which may lend this project significant political clout.

Barriers to the Bio-fuel Industry in India

Although bio-fuels may be a good energy alternative option in the future, there are a lot of barriers that keep the Indian bio-fuel industry from getting off the ground in the present. Experts from all over the world have a spectrum of opinions about the most important barriers that prevent the bio-fuel industry from growing rapidly. The following are a few major stumbling blocks.

From a logistical standpoint, India is not ready to invest heavily in fuels because the political and physical infrastructure necessary to support the industry currently does not exist. Although the Indian government proposed the National Mission on

Bio-fuels in 2003, the government still lacks the political backing to realistically implement a programme of that magnitude. The Mission provides governmental suggestion on developing the bio-fuel industry. However, there is little policy to make sure these guidelines are followed. Moreover, the physical infrastructure to support a proposed bio-fuel industry of that size is lacking. While there are a significant number of industrial plants that can process bio-ethanol, there are very few capable of producing bio-diesel. In India, the demand for diesel is over five times higher than the demand for petrol. Thus, if India is serious about bio-diesel from jatropha or other oilseed plants, it must invest significantly in acquiring additional and advanced technologies in oil extraction, transesterification, and storage for bio-diesel oil. For example, prior to 2006, there were no transesterification plants capable of producing commercial bio-diesel. Now, there are only a handful of transesterification plants in operation and they do not operate at full capacity. India needs to scale up its efforts drastically if it hopes to produces fuels with 20 per cent bio-fuel by 2017.

There are environmental barriers and concerns to large-scale bio-fuel production and use in India. The availability of both land and already scarce water resources may greatly limit bio-fuels. Currently, it takes 3,500 liters of irrigation water to produce one liter of ethanol from sugarcane. Many experts say that as a result, India must look to drought resistant crops such as jatropha to avoid enormous water shortages as a result of bio-fuels. However, it is unclear how much water jatropha needs to produce its maximum yield. If jatropha requires a significant amount of irrigation to reach its potential, it is almost assured that water shortages will increase in frequency. It is also possible that the bio-fuel industry's demand for water would take water away from food production, which could further exacerbate food insecurity in India. Additionally, it is still unclear whether or not bio-diesel from jatropha will help decrease India's greenhouse gas emissions. Jatropha may be a source or a sink for greenhouse gases depending on numerous factors such as its efficiency in taking up carbon dioxide (which still remains unknown) and the amount of fossil fuels burned to process jatropha into bio-diesel (which will depend on the technology and processes used).

On a more local level, the bio-fuel industry is hindered by Indian farmers' lack of confidence in bio-fuels. In order to enlarge the bio-fuel industry at a significant rate, the Indian government needs to find a way to show that it is serious about the bio-fuel industry and that it is ready to support small and large farmers' investments. The government has begun to do so by establishing Minimum Support Prices and Minimum Purchase Prices. However, it needs to continue to find new ways to convince farmers to invest.

The Future of Bio-fuels

In light of the fact that commercial bio-fuel production and use is a relatively new concept, all stakeholders – including the Indian government, small farmers, investors, and researchers — have an array of possible actions and stances regarding bio-fuels. There are numerous different opinions about what the logical next steps are. The following are a few potential options for India.

Much research is undoubtedly necessary to better understand the capabilities and downfalls of bio-fuels. A huge number of questions remain and more are still surfacing. For example, whether jatropha will be economically viable compared to oil, whether indirect and environmental costs of bio-fuels will outweigh the direct benefits, or whether impoverished farmers will significantly benefit, all are still unanswered. Some believe that research needs to come before the Indian government invests major sums into bio-fuel development policy particularly those policies based around jatropha. Others have indicated that India must work to improve its agricultural practices before it moves forward with the rest of its bio-fuel agenda.

There are improvements the government could start making in order to give the bio-fuel industry a solid support system from which it can grow. Advances in agriculture through water saving methods, intercropping, seasonal planting, and crop rotation could create more efficiency in the agricultural sector and therefore increase yields. These improvements could create a variety of positive effects downstream in the bio-fuel industry and the rest of Indian society.

Investing time and money studying and domesticating jatropha also has potential benefits. The Indian government has indicated through its policies and public statements that it hopes to make jatropha a central part of the bio-fuel industry. Unfortunately, however, there still is not enough information about jatropha to ensure that the Indian government would get a substantial return on its investment.

Case Study 2

Case Name: Indian Council for Enviro-Legal Action vs. Union of India

Court Name: Supreme Court of India, New Delhi, India

Writ Petition (C) No. 967 of 1989

Year: 18 July, 2011

Introduction

This writ petition filed by an environmentalist organization Indian Council for Enviro-Legal Action brings to light the woes of people living in the vicinity of chemical industrial plants in Bichhri Village in particular (and in general across the country India). The case highlights the disregard, nay, contempt for law and lawful authorities on the part of some among the emerging breed of entrepreneurs, taking advantage, as they do, of the country's need for industrialization and export earnings. Quest of profit has extremely drained them of any feeling for the fellow human beings – for that matter, for anything else. And the law seems to have been helpless; Systemic Defects? It is such instance, which has led many people in this country to believe that disregard of law pays and that the consequences of such disregard will never be visited upon them – particularly, if they are men with means. Bichhri is a small village located in the Udaipur District of Rajasthan, India. North of this village, there are major industrial establishment, Hindustan Zinc Limited, a public sector concern.

However, it did not affect Bichhri but the problems began in 1987 when the fourth respondent herein, Hindustan Agro Chemicals Limited started producing certain chemicals like Oleum (said to be the concentrated form of sulphuric acid) and Single Super Phosphate. The real calamity occurred when another sister concern, Silver Chemicals (Respondent 5), commenced production of "H" acid in a plant located within the same complex. "H" acid was meant for export exclusively. Its manufacture gives rise to enormous quantities of highly toxic effluents in particular, iron-based and gypsum-based sludge – which if not properly treated, pose grave threat to Mother Earth. It poisons the earth, the water and everything that comes in contact with it. Jyoti Chemicals (Respondent 8) is another unit established to produce "H" acid, besides some other chemicals. Respondents 6 and 7 were established to produce fertilizers and a few other products.

All the units/factories of Respondents 4 to 8 are situated in the same geographic region and are controlled by the same group of individuals. All the units are what may be called "chemical industries".

As per the report, about 2500 tonnes of highly toxic sludge was produced while producing 375 tonnes of H-acid. And, all these sludge thrown in the open field of village area. Over period of time, the toxic chemicals leached and percolated deep into the ground and polluted the aquifers and subterranean supply of water. The water of the wells and other streams in the vicinity turned dark in colour and became polluted very badly. It did not remain for any use including drinking, irrigation, and cattle. The soil has become polluted rendering it unfit for cultivation, which is the main source of livelihood for the villagers. Further, the pollution caused disease, death and disaster in the village and in the nearby areas. This sudden degradation of earth and water had an echo in Parliament also and the respective Minister ensured that the action was taken, but nothing meaningful was done on the spot. The villagers then rose in virtual revolt leading to the imposition of Section 144 of the Criminal Procedure Code by the District Magistrate in the area and the closure of Silver Chemicals in January, 1989.

Procedural History

The Indian Council for Environ-Legal Action filed the Writ Petition in August, 1989 with the prayer to the Court that appropriate remedial action need to be initiated. The Rajasthan Pollution Control Board in its affidavit stated that: (i) the Hindustan Agro Chemicals Ltd. obtained NOC from the Board for manufacturing sulphuric acid and alumina sulphate. But this unit changed its products without clearance from the Board and started manufacturing oleum and single super phosphate. The consent was refused and directions were issued under the Air (Prevention and Control of Pollution) Act, 1981 to close down the unit; and (ii) the Silver Chemical stated to be manufacturing of H-acid without obtaining NOC from the Board. The waste produced from the manufacturing of H-acid was highly acidic and contained very high concentration of dissolved solids along with several other pollutants. Likewise, the detail report was submitted by the every concern Board and Authority to the Hon'ble Supreme Court for the consideration. Further, the Government of Rajasthan filed its counter-affidavit on 20-1-1990. It made a curious statement in Para 3 to the following effect: that the State Government is now aware of the pollution of undergroundwater being caused by liquid effluents from the firms arrayed as Respondents 4 to 8 in the writ petition. Therefore, the State Government has initiated action through the Pollution Control Board to check further spread of pollution. The Hon'ble Court asked the National Environmental Engineering Research Institute (NEERI) to study the situation in and around Bichhri village and submit their report "as to the choice and scale of the available remedial alternatives". NEERI was also requested to suggest both short-term and long-term measures required to combat the hazard already caused. Based on the NEERI report and other evidences, Supreme Court directed that the sludge lying on the land be removed immediately to avoid the risk of seepage of toxic substances into the soil during the rainy season. On April 4, 1990, the Court further directed the Ministry of Environment and Forests, Government of India to depute its experts immediately to inspect the area to ascertain the existence and extent of gypsum-based and iron-based sludge and to suggest the handling and disposal procedures and to prescribe a package for its transportation and safe storage. The cost of such storage and transportation was directed to be recovered from the industries located in the Complex. However, on February 13, 1996, Supreme Court passed the final order as: "they are in the view that if an enterprise which is engaged in a hazardous or inherent industry which possess a potential threat to the health and safety of the persons working in the factory and residing in the surrounding areas, it is an absolute and non-delegable duty to the community to ensure that no harm to any one on account of hazardous or inherently dangerous nature of activity which it has undertaken. It is, therefore, held that where an enterprise is engaged in a hazardous or inherently dangerous activity and harm to any one on account of an accident, the enterprise is strictly and absolutely liable to compensate all those who are affected by the accident and such liability is not subject to any of the exceptions as laid down in tortuous principles of strict liability under the rule laid down in Rylands versus Flecher. The law laid down in the case of Oleum Gas Leak case (M.C. Mehta v. UOI and Ors) is also applicable in the present case and the industries are absolutely liable to compensate for the harm caused by them to the villagers in the affected area, to the soil and to the groundwater and hence they are bound to take all necessary measures to remove the sludge and other pollutants lying in the affected area which is about 350 hectares. The polluter pays principle demands that the financial cost of preventing or remedying damage caused by pollution should lie with the industries which caused the pollution".

However, this is a very unusual and extraordinary litigation where even after fifteen years of the final judgment of this Court (date of judgment February 13, 1996), the litigation has been deliberately kept alive by filing one interlocutory application or the other in order to avoid compliance of the judgment. The said judgment of this Court has not been permitted to acquire finality till date. This is a classic example how by abuse of the process of law even the final judgment of the Supreme Court can be circumvented for more than a decade. This is undeniably a very serious matter concerning the sanctity and integrity of the judicial system in general and of the Supreme Court of the country in particular.

> Mr. M.C. Mehta, Advocate has filed written submissions on behalf of Indian Council for Enviro-Legal Action. It is reiterated in the submissions that these applications are blatant disregard towards complying with the directions of this Court. They have made mockery with the environmental justice delivery system by filing these applications. They have shown no contrition for causing irreparable damage to the life, health and property of the people affected by their commercial activities. The applicants are trying to delay the payment of ₹ 373,850,000 INR for carrying out remedial measures. Mr. Mehta also placed reliance on a judgment of this Court in the case of M.C. Mehta v. Kamal Nath andothers (2000) 6 SCC 213, in which the Court observed as under: and quote; ...pollution is a civil wrong. By its very nature, it is a tort committed against the community as a whole. A person, therefore, who is guilty of causing pollution, has to pay damages (compensation) for restoration of the environment and ecology. He has also to pay damages to those who have suffered loss on account of the act of the offender. The powers of this Court under Articles 32 and 21 are not restricted and it can award damages in a PIL or a Writ Petition as has been held in a series of decisions. In addition to damages aforesaid, the person guilty of causing pollution can also be held liable to pay exemplary damages so that it may act as a deterrent for others not to cause pollution in any manner.

Issues

(i) What is the measure of liability of companies which are engaged in a hazardous or inherently dangerous industry, if by reason of an accident occurring in such industry, persons die or are injured?

(ii) Does the rule in Rylands v. Fletcher apply in such case or is there any other principle on which the liability can be determined?

(iii) The respondents must pay the amount necessary to carry out appropriate remedial action is one thing but should they pay only that amount or with interest? If the period were a few days or months that would have been different but in this case, it is almost14 years have been lapsed and amount has not been paid

In fact, it involves three questions:

(a) Can a party who does not comply with the court order be permitted to retain the benefits of his own wrong of non-compliance?

(b) Whether the successful party be not compensated by way of restitution for deprivation of its legitimate dues for more than fourteen years? and

(c) Whether the court should not remove all incentives for not complying with the judgment of the court?

Reasoning

(i) The concern companies have strict liability by following the rule in Rylands v. Fletcher.

(ii) The rule in Rylands v. Fletcher was evolved in 1866 and it provides that a person who for his own purposes brings on to his land and collects and keeps there anything likely to do mischief if it escapes must keep it at his peril and, if he fails to do so, is *prima facie* liable for the damage which is the natural consequence of its escape. The liability under this rule is strict and it is no defence that the thing escaped without that person's wilful act, default or neglect or even that he had no knowledge of its existence. This rule laid down a principle of liability that if a person who brings on to his land and collects and keeps there anything likely to do harm and such thing escapes and does damage to another, he is liable to compensate for the damage caused. Of course, this rule applies only to non-natural user of the land and it does not apply to things naturally on the land or where the escape is due to an act of God and an act of a stranger or the default of the person injured or where the thing which escapes is present by the consent of the person injured or in certain cases where there is statutory authority.

(iii) It is settled principle of law that no one can take advantage of his own wrong unless courts disgorge all benefits that a party availed by obstruction or delays or non-compliance. There will always be incentive for non-compliance, and parties are ingenious enough to come up with all kinds of pleas and other tactics to achieve their end because they know that in the end the benefit will remain with them. Thus, whatever benefits a person has had or could have had by not complying with the judgment must be disgorged and paid to the judgment creditor and not allowed to be retained by the judgment-debtor. This is the bounden duty and obligation of the Court.

Analysis (Constitutional Provisions)

- Article 48A (added after 42 Amendment, 1976) of the Indian Constitution states that "the State shall endeavour to protect and improve the environment and to safeguard the forest and wildlife of the country."
- Article 51A(g) entitled as "Fundamental Duties", imposes a similar responsibility on every citizen "to protect and improve the natural environment including forests, lakes, rivers and wild life, and to have compassion for living creature".
- Further, the Interpretation given by the Supreme Court in Maneka Gandhi case has added new dimensions to the concept of personal liberty of an individual. It laid down that a law affecting life and liberty of a person has to stand the scrutiny of Articles 14 and 19 of the Constitution. In other words, if a law is enacted by a legislature which touches upon the life and liberty of a person and curtails it, then it is a mandatory requirement that the procedure established by it for curtailing the liberty of a person must be reasonable, fair and just. It is this interpretation of Article 21 which the Court has extended further so as to include the right to a wholesome environment. Likewise, environmental pollution which spoils the atmosphere and thereby affects the life and health of the person has been regarded as amounting to violation of Article 21 of the

Constitution. In Dehradun Quarry's case, the Supreme Court entertained complaints from the rural litigation and entitlement Kendra, Dehradun alleging that the operations of limestone quarries in the Mussoorie-Dehradun region resulted in degradation of the environment affecting the fragile ecosystems in the area. In this case, the Supreme Court moving under Article 32 ordered the closure of some of these quarries on the ground that these were upsetting the ecological balance. Though, the judgment did not make a reference to Article 21 but involving of jurisdiction by the court under Article 32 presupposed the violation of right to life guaranteed under Article 21.

- Article 32 of the Indian Constitution gives exclusive privilege to every Indian citizen to file a petition whose fundamental right is violated by any means and by any one.

  So, in this case, the Supreme Court under Articles 48-A and 21 of the Constitution regarded the right to live in a healthy environment as a part of life and personal liberty of the people.

Further, through, Environment (Protection) Act, 1986, the power has been conferred upon the Central Government for laying down the standards for the quality of air, water and soil. It is hoped that this will ensure uniformity of standards throughout the country. However, if any issue or dispute arises, then of course the Constitution has given enough provisions to judiciary under which it can take substantial step. In recent time, the Supreme Court of India has played a vital role and has been giving directions from time to time to the administrative authorities to take necessary steps for improving the environment. Public Interest Litigation and Judicial Activism are the wonderful tools to ensure the environmental rights and environmental conservation.

Decision

July 18, 2011, Justice Bhandari Dalveer and Dattu H.L.: " We have carefully considered the facts and circumstances of this case. We have also considered the law declared by this Court and by other countries in a number of cases. We are clearly of the opinion that the concerned applicant industry must deposit the amount as directed by this Court vide order dated April 11, 1997 with compound interest. The applicant industry has deliberately not complied with the orders of this court since April 11, 1997. Thousands of villagers have been adversely affected because no effective remedial steps have been taken so far. The applicant industry has succeeded in their design in not complying with the Court's order by keeping the litigation alive for more than 15 years by filing the interlocutory applications which were being totally devoid of any merit are accordingly dismissed with costs. Consequently, the applicant industry is directed to pay ₹ 37,385,000 INR (USD 608,628) along with compound interest @ 12 per cent per annum from April 11, 1997 till the amount is paid or recovered. The applicant industry is also directed to pay costs of litigation. Even after final judgment of this Court, the litigation has been kept alive for almost 15 years. The respondents have been compelled to defend this litigation for all these years. Enormous Court's time has been wasted for all these years. On consideration of the totality of the facts and circumstances of this case, we direct the applicant industry to pay costs of ₹ 1,000,000 INR (USD 16,280) in both the Interlocutory Applications. The amount of costs would also be utilized for carrying out remedial measure in village Bichhri and surrounding areas in Udaipur District of Rajasthan, India on the direction of the concerned authorities".

Conclusion

Moreover, this Court applied the principle of Polluter Pays and observed thus: the polluter pays principle demands that the financial costs of preventing or remedying damage caused by pollution should lie with the undertakings which caused the pollution, or produced the goods which caused the pollution. Under this principle, it is not the role of government to meet the costs involved in either prevention of such damage, or in carrying out remedial action, because the effect of this would be to shift the financial burden of the pollution incident to the taxpayer.

This case study is adopted from https://www.academia.edu/5402800/Environmental-law-case-study

CHECK YOUR UNDERSTANDING

1. What are the issues in management of ethics?
2. Briefly explain Hosmer Model
3. Give some instances of ethical dilemma. How such situations are resolved?
4. What is code of ethics and explain its utility?
5. Are environmental legislations adequate in India?
6. What is the level of acceptance of environmental ethics in India?

REFERENCES

1. Fernando A.C.: Business Environment, Pearson Education, New Delhi.
2. Gupta, C.B.: Business Ethics and Communication, Sultan Chand & Sons.
3. https://www.academia.edu/5402800/Environmental-law-case-study

Chapter 4 Legal Aspects of Ethics

This Chapter deals with:

- Politico-legal Environment
- Constitutional Provisions Relating to Business
- Political Setup and Implications for Business
- Prominent Features of MRTP, FERA and FEMA
- Socio-cultural Environment and Impact on Business

INTRODUCTION

The business firm does not operate in a vacuum but in a given environment and has to interact and transact its business within this environment. A business organization is a microeconomic unit influenced by its environment – both economic and non-economic; internal and external; the laws enacted by the government; the rules governing the economy; economic policies that include monetary, fiscal and commercial policies laid down for its observation and follow-up. Therefore, the business environment and the manner and the effectiveness of the interaction of an enterprise with its environment would generally determine its success or failure.

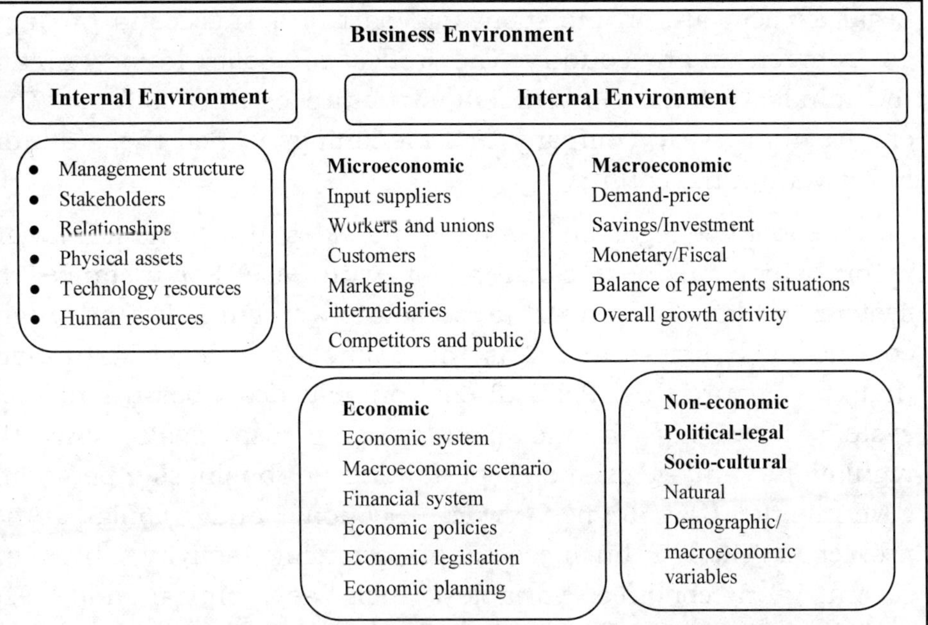

Figure 4.1: Factors that Affect a Business Environment

Figure 4.1 depicts the components of business environment. In this Chapter, we will examine the impact of politico-legal and socio-cultural factors on business. These two form part of non-economic factors.

POLITICO-LEGAL ENVIRONMENT

By politico-legal environment is meant the situation and circumstances relating to the government, politics and public affairs of a country. They also relate to the laws, the government agencies that implement them and pressure groups that influence and limit various organizations and individuals. In recent times, there is a tremendous increase in the number of business legislations and growth of special interest groups, especially with reference to environmental activities. For raising revenue and for other reasons, governments impose various types of taxes on business firms, households and individuals. In almost all countries, business enterprises are directly or indirectly required to pay heavier taxes not only to defray the expenses of the government, but also to carry out social welfare programmes for the benefit of the poor and underprivileged sections of the society.

Legal aspects are an indispensable part of a successful business environment in any country. They reflect the policy framework and the mindset of the Government structure of that country. They ensure that every company is functioning as per the statutory framework of the country.

The politico-legal environment provides the legal framework within which business can function with ease. For instance, the system and laws of contract are absolutely essential for the orderly conduct of business and it is the political and legal institutions that can ensure this. Political environment describes the political system prevailing in the country and also deals with the regulations and legislations pertaining to business operations, government programmes, war, election, and similar other problems. Though business is an economic activity, there are several non-economic variables such as political and legal environment which influence its sphere of activity.

There are as many legal systems as there are countries, and in many cases, states, cities or provinces also have their own laws. The politico-legal constrains deal more with the activities and decisions, of the firms. Laws may prevent firms from doing something or require them to do something else. Thus, a labour law may prohibit the company from using teenage workers in certain jobs and staffing may be somewhat different from what it might otherwise be.

INDIAN CONSTITUTION AND BUSINESS

The Constitution of India has guaranteed some fundamental rights to the citizens and has also laid down certain directive principles of State policy for the achievement of a social order based on justice, liberty, equality and fraternity. The Constitution is a comprehensive one consisting of various provisions that affect every citizen of India. Certain provisions of the Indian Constitution are applicable to the business which are summarized under the following headings:

Preamble of Constitution and Business

The Indian Constitution starts with a Preamble, which outlines the main objectives of the Constitution. It may be noted that though the Preamble is not a part of the Constitution and is not justifiable, yet its significance cannot be denied. It serves as a key to the Constitution. Whenever the judiciary is in doubt about any particular provision of the Constitution, it refers to the preamble to find out the real intentions of the framers of the Constitution. The Preamble reads:

"We, the people of India, have solemnly resolved to constitute India into a Sovereign, Socialist, and Secular Democratic Republic and to secure to all its citizens:

Justice, social, economic and political; liberty of thought, expression, belief, faith and worship; equality of status and of opportunity; and to promote among them all fraternity assuring the dignity of the individual and the unity and integrity of the nation."

A perusal of the Preamble shows that it intends India to be a Sovereign, Socialist, Secular, and Democratic Republic. It means that like other states India is a sovereign state and is free to conduct its internal as well as external relations as it deems desirable.

Democratic government implies the Government is to be carried on by the elected representatives of the people, and the Government stays in office as long as it enjoys the confidence of their elected representatives. Republic implies that the highest executive authority in India shall vest in a person directly elected by the people. In other words, there is no place for monarchical or feudal system in India.

Fundamental Rights and Business

The Indian Constitution incorporates a list of Fundamental Rights and guarantees their inviolability by executive and legislative authorities. Part III (Articles 12-35) deals with the Fundamental Rights granted to individuals. These rights were finalized by the Committee of the Constituent Assembly headed by Sardar Vallabhbhai Patel.

The six types of fundamental rights of the Constitution are as follows:

1. **Right to Equality (Articles 14 to 18):** Articles 14 to 18 deal with right to equality. The Constitution clearly provides that the State shall not deny to any person equality before law or the equal protection of law within the territory of India. It cannot discriminate against any citizen on grounds of religion, race, caste, sex, and place of birth or any of them.

   It means that every citizen has access to shops, public restaurants, hotels, places of public entertainment etc. and is free to use wells, tanks, roads and places of public resort maintained at State funds.

2. **Right to Freedom (Articles 19 to 22):** Articles 19 to 22 enumerates certain positive rights conferred by the Constitution in order to promote the ideal of liberty promised in the Preamble. Six fundamental rights in the nature of 'freedom' are guaranteed to the citizens in the article The six freedoms are as follows:

   (i) Freedom of speech and expression.

   (ii) Freedom of peaceful assembly without arms.

   (iii) Freedom of association.

   (iv) Freedom of movement throughout the territory of India.

   (v) Freedom to reside or settle any part of the territory.

   (vi) Freedom to practise any profession, or to carry on any occupation, trade or business.

   The right to freedom is also applied equally in business. The businessmen can express their problems freely to the government and can get a solution to it. Similarly, every citizen has the right to choose any business or profession and can form unions, and conduct meetings.

3. **Right against Exploitation (Articles 23 to 24):** Articles 23 to 24 deal with the right against exploitation and seek to prevent exploitation of weaker sections of society by unscrupulous persons as well as the State. Article 23 prohibits traffic in human beings, involuntary work without payment and other forms of forced labour. Article 24 prohibits the employment of children below 14 years of age in factories and hazardous occupations, employing women employees in night shifts in factories etc.

   Economic Importance:

   The economic importance of right against exploitation is:

   (i) The government takes necessary steps to remove bonded labour.

   (ii) The Factories Act help to prevent exploitation of women and children employees.

   (iii) The owner of the factories are guided to make provision for safety and welfare of the workers and they compulsorily appoint a labour welfare officer, if in the factory 500 or more workers are employed.

4. **Right to Freedom of Religion (Articles 25 to 28):** Articles 25 to 28 deal with the right to freedom of religion. Subject to public order, morality, health etc., the citizens enjoy freedom of conscience and are free to profess, practise and propagate any religion.

   However, the State can regulate or restrict the economic, financial, political or other secular activities associated with religious practices. No citizen can be compelled to pay any taxes the proceeds of which are to be spent for the promotion or maintenance of any particular religion or religious domination.

   Economic Importance:

   The economic importance of the right to freedom of religion is:

   (i) The government cannot spend tax money for the development of any religion.

(ii) Nobody can be compelled to pay tax for the welfare of any specific religion.

(iii) No one shall be forced to transfer of property or any agreement of a business nature in the name of a particular religion.

5. **Cultural and Educational Rights (Articles 29 to 30):** Article 29 stipulates that the State shall not impose upon it any culture other than the community's own culture. A minority community has the right to preserve its culture and religious interests. Article 30 confers upon a minority community the right to establish and administer educational institutions of its choice.

   A notable feature of the educational and cultural right is that unlike other fundamental rights, it is not subject to any restriction, except that the State can make special provisions for the advancement of any socially and educationally backward classes of citizens.

   Economic Importance:

   The economic importance of cultural and educational rights are:

   (i) The State does not discriminate to give economic assistance to the minority institutions.

   (ii) The aided institution cannot refuse admission to any of the citizens on the ground that he belongs to a particular caste, religion, language or region.

6. **Right to Constitutional Remedies (Article 32):** This right has been described by Dr. Ambedkar as the 'heart and soul' of the Constitution. In tact, the mere declaration of fundamental rights is useless unless effective remedies are available for their enforcement. This has been ensured under Article 32 which grants the right to move the Supreme Court by appropriate proceedings for the enforcement of the rights conferred by the Constitution.

   Clause (2) of Article 32 confers power on the supreme court to issue appropriate directions or orders to writs, including writs in the name of habeas corpus, mandamas, prohibition, quo-warrant and certiorari for the enforcement of any of the rights conferred by Part III of the Constitution.

Thus, the fundamental rights enumerated in the constitution guarantee a number of economic and social rights to the citizens. At the same time, the State has the power to impose reasonable restrictions on such rights in the interest of the people.

DIRECTIVE PRINCIPLES OF STATE POLICY

The Directive Principles of State Policy which have been enshrined in Part IV of the Constitution aim at realizing the high ideals of justice, liberty, equality and fraternity as outlined in the Preamble to the Constitution. There are ideas which are to inspire the State to work for the common good of the people and establish social and economic democracy in the country.

The phrase 'Directive Principles of State Policy' means the principles which the states should keep in mind while framing the laws and formulating policy. Articles 39 to 51 contain the various directive principles. These principles are amalgamation of socialistic, Gandhian and liberal principles.

Economic Importance

The economic importance of Directive Principles of State Policy is:

(i) To provide adequate means of livelihood for all the citizens.

(ii) To secure equal pay for work to both men and women.

(iii) To protect the workers, especially children.

(iv) To regulate the economic system of the country that it does not lead to concentration of wealth and means of production.

(v) To make provision for securing right to work, to education and to public assistance in cases of unemployment, old age, sickness and similar other cases.

(vi) To ensure a decent standard of living and facilities of leisure for all workers.

The main objective of the above noted directive principles is to enable the individual to lead a good and satisfying life. All the provisions of directive principles of State policy guide the government policies towards the business and other economic and social activities.

The government also so far enacted a number of acts and laws policies and rules keeping in view the directive principles, which are directly related with the business operations. The various Acts like FERA, Factories Act. MRTP Act, Minimum Wages Act, Industrial (Development and Regulation) Act, Industrial Policy, etc. are based on the Directive Principles of the Constitution.

The government, through these acts and regulations, protects the interests of working men, women and children, prevents concentration of economic power, and promotes and protects the interest of small and cottage industries.

CONSTITUTIONAL PROVISIONS REGARDING TRADE AND COMMERCE WITHIN THE TERRITORY OF INDIA

Articles 301 to 307 of Constitution of India deals with the constitutional provisions regarding trade and commerce. The framers of the Indian Constitution were fully conscious of the importance of maintaining the economic unity of the Union of India.

Free movement and exchange of goods throughout the territory of India was essential for the economic unity of the country which alone could sustain the progress of the country.

Prior to the integration of India and enforcement of the new Constitution, there were in existence a large number of Indian states which in exercise of their sovereign powers, had created customs barriers between themselves and the rest of India, thus hindering at several points which constituted the boundaries of those Indian states, the free flow of commerce.

Thus, the main object of Article 301 was obviously to encouraging the free flow of stream of trade and commerce throughout the territory of India. The word 'trade' means 'buying' or 'selling' of goods while the term 'commerce' includes all forms of transportation such as by land, air or water.

Article 302 of Indian Constitution explains the power of Parliament to impose restrictions on trade, commerce and intercourse. The Parliament may by law impose it. Such restrictions on the freedom of trade, commerce or intercourse between one state and another or within any part of the territory of India, as may be required in the public interest.

Article 303 deals with the restrictions on the legislative powers of the Union and of the States with regard to trade and commerce. It provides that Parliament shall not have power to make any law giving any preference to any one State over another by virtue of any entry relating to trade and commerce in any one of the list in the VIIth Schedule. But under Clause (2) of this article, the Parliament may however, discriminate among states. It is declared by a law that it is necessary to do so for the purpose of dealing with the situation arising from scarcity of goods in any part of the territory of India. The question whether there is a scarcity of goods in any part of India is for the Parliament to decide.

Article 304 explains State's power to regulate trade and commerce. The details, (a) impose on goods imported from other states (or the Union Territories) any tax to which similar goods manufactured or produced in that State are subject and (b) impose such reasonable restrictions on the freedom of trade, commerce or intercourse with or within that state as may be required in the public interest.

Article 305 saves existing laws and laws providing for State monopolies insofar as the President may by order otherwise direct. Article 307 empowers Parliament to appoint such authority as it considers appropriate for carrying out for purposes of Articles 301, 302, 303 and 304. It can confer on such authorities such powers and duties as it thinks necessary

Different commercial and industrial laws have been enacted to play very important role in regulation of economic activities and creating conductive environment for successful operations of business and industries:

- Indian Companies Act, 1956
- Indian Partnership Act 1932
- Negotiable Instrument Act , 1881
- Indian Contract Act, 1872
- The Sale of Goods Act, 1920
- The Carriers Act, 1865

Indian Companies Act, 1956: It empowers the Central Government to regulate the formation, financing, functioning and winding up of companies. The Act contains the mechanism regarding organizational, financial, managerial and all the relevant aspects of a company. It provides for the powers and responsibilities of the directors and managers, raising of capital, holding of company meetings, maintenance and audit of company accounts, powers of inspection, etc. The Act applies to whole of India and to all types of companies.

Indian Partnership Act, 1932: It empowers the Central Government to regulate the formation, financing, functioning and winding up of companies. The Act contains the mechanism regarding organizational, financial, managerial and all the relevant aspects of a company. It provides for the powers and responsibilities of the directors and managers, raising of capital, holding of company meetings, maintenance and audit of company accounts, powers of inspection, etc. The Act applies to whole of India and to all types of companies.

Negotiable Instrument Act, 1881: A Negotiable Instrument means a promissory note, bill of exchange or cheque payable either to order or to bearer. These instruments facilitate the business.

Indian Contract Act, 1872: The Indian Contract Act, 1872 is the governing legislation for contracts, which lays down the general principles relating to formation, performance and enforceability of contracts and the rules relating to certain special types of contracts like Indemnity and Guarantee, Bailment and Pledge, and Agency.

The Sale of Goods Act, 1930: Law relating to the sale of goods is a branch of contract law which is applicable to contracts for the sale of goods such as offer and its acceptance, capacity of parties, free consent, consideration and legality of the object. It applies only to movables other than actionable claims and money.

The Carriers Act, 1865: According to the Act, common carriers denotes a person, other than government, engaged in the business of transport document or of transporting for hire. They can be made responsible for transporting goods if public is ready to pay for freight, etc.

Law of Industrial Relations: It has also greatly influenced the trade union movement in our country. Industrial relations operate in a legal system. It is an extent to which it attempts to regulate relationships. It is obligatory rather than optional.

Legal aspect of business empowers the government to intervene in business activities. The basic purpose of this intervention is to protect the interest of workers employed in the industries and other similar institutions. Fundamental rights and directive principles of State policies as given in Indian Constitution expect that the government should take initiative to safeguard the interest of labour.

POLITICAL SETUP – MAJOR CHARACTERISTICS AND THEIR IMPLICATIONS FOR BUSINESS

Political setup refers to political, government and legal institutions. It has close relationship with the economic system and economic policy. In communist countries, laws control investment and related matters.

There are number of laws that regulate the conduct of the business. These laws cover matters such as standards of business and its production or service. In democratic countries, laws/acts are passed by the Parliament. Then they are regarded rules and regulations of business according to the Act.

Some of the implications are given below:

- Political stability, responsibility, political ideology and level of political morality, the law and order situation, and practice of the ruling party and major purposes and efficiency of the government agencies. political agency's nature, its influence to economic and industrial activities in the country impact business.
- Government policies like fiscal, monetary, industrial, labour and export and import policies which are influenced by specific legal enactments.
- The political environment is based on the uncertainty, therefore, democratic countries consist of many political parties. If a party does not get majority to form a government, in such situation the industry and business collapse due to hung mandate. It affects the policy formulation process. Therefore, a stable government is required for business to prosper.
- The government policies rules and regulations control and monitor the business enterprises and its activities in the State.
- The type of government administration of the State and business policy create the business atmosphere.
- The Government tax policy is critical and affect the business organizations in the State.
- Sound legal system is the basic requirement for running of the business operating in the State.
- Various business laws which are protecting the consumer, competitors, and organizations impact business.
- Political system also influence business and its activities.
- Political pressure groups influence the government which in turn regulate the business to some extent within the country.

- Special interest groups and political action committee put pressure on business organization to pay more attention to consumer rights, minority rights and rights of women.
- Sporadic movement against certain products and services also affect the business organizations.

PROMINENT FEATURES OF MRTP, FERA AND FEMA

The MRTP Act 1969

It was the stated policy of Government of India in the early period of its pursuing the path of rapid industrialization to curb monopolies and monopolistic practices. The most important step towards the curbing of monopolies was the passing of the Monopolies and Restrictive Trade Practices Act, in 1969.

A monopoly is said to exist where at least one person or a company controls one-third of a local or national market. In many countries, the attitude of the public towards complete and partial monopolies for many years has been mainly due to the abuses of monopoly which include: (i) high prices and restricted output; (ii) wrong allocation of resources; (iii) abuse of investors by monopolists, painting alluring pictures of high profits and perpetual exploitation of the market and (iv) preventing inventions since a monopolist's profits do not depend upon continuous progress in production. It is for these reasons that monopoly has been regarded as a social evil and various measure have been designed in free-enterprise economies to control and regulate it or in some cases to eliminate it altogether. Competition is, thus, considered to be the best market practice what will benefit consumers. Two pieces of legislation that were designed and implemented keeping in mind the larger goals of the State – The MRTP Act and the Competition Act are discussed below.

The objectives of MRTP Act, 1969 was:

(i) To ensure prohibition of monopolies and unfair trade practices

(ii) To ensure that there is no concentration of economic power to the common detriment, and control of monopolies.

Salient Features of MRTP Act 1969

The Salient features of MRTP Act, 1969 were:

- A restrictive trade practice is a trade practice, which:
  - (i) Prevents, distorts or restricts competition in any manner or
  - (ii) Obstructs the flow of capital or resources into the stream of production; or
  - (iii) Which tends to bring about manipulation of prices, imposing on the consumers unjustified cost or restrictions.
- The Commission may inquire into any restrictive trade practice:
  - (i) Upon receiving a complaint from any trade association, consumer or a registered consumer association, or
  - (ii) Upon a reference made to it by the Central or State Government or
  - (iii) Upon its own knowledge or information
- The Commission shall if after making an inquiry it is of the opinion that the practice is prejudicial to the public interest it may direct that:
  - (i) The practice shall be discontinued or shall not be repeated;
  - (ii) The agreement relating thereto shall be void in respect of such restrictive trade practice or shall stand modified.
  - (iii) The Commission may permit the party to any restrictive trade practice to take steps so that it is no longer prejudicial to the public interest

Unfair Trade Practice

An unfair trade practice means a trade practice, which, for the purpose of promoting any sale, use or supply of any goods or services, adopts unfair method, or unfair or deceptive practice.

Unfair practices may be categorised as under:

1. **False Representation:** The practice of making any oral or written statement or representation which:
   - (i) Falsely suggests that the goods are of a particular standard quality, quantity, grade, composition, style or model;
   - (ii) Falsely suggests that the services are of a particular standard, quantity or grade;
   - (iii) Falsely suggests any re-built, second-hand renovated, reconditioned or old goods as new goods;
   - (iv) Represents that the goods or services have sponsorship, approval, performance, characteristics, accessories, uses or benefits which they do not have;
   - (v) Represents that the seller or the supplier has a sponsorship or approval or affiliation which he does not have;
   - (vi) Makes a false or misleading representation concerning the need for, or the usefulness of, any goods or services;
   - (vii) Gives any warranty or guarantee of the performance, efficacy or length of life of the goods, that is not based on an adequate or proper test;
   - (viii) Makes to the public a representation in the form that purports to be—
     - A warranty or guarantee of the goods or services,
     - A promise to replace, maintain or repair the goods until it has achieved a specified result,

     if such representation is materially misleading or there is no reasonable prospect that such warranty, guarantee or promise will be fulfilled;
   - (ix) Materially misleads about the prices at which such goods or services are available in the market; or
   - (x) Gives false or misleading facts disparaging the goods, services or trade of another person.
2. **False Offer of Bargain Price:** Where an advertisement is published in a newspaper or otherwise, whereby goods or services are offered at a bargain price when in fact there is

no intention that the same may be offered at that price, for a reasonable period or reasonable quantity, it shall amount to an unfair trade practice.

The bargain price, for this purpose means—

(i) The price stated in the advertisement in such manner as suggests that it is lesser than the ordinary price, or

(ii) The price which any person coming across the advertisement would believe to be better than the price at which such goods are ordinarily sold.

3. **Free Gifts Offer and Prize Schemes:** The unfair trade practices under this category are:

(i) Offering any gifts, prizes or other items along with the goods when the real intention is different, or

(ii) Creating impression that something is being offered free along with the goods, when in fact the price is wholly or partly covered by the price of the article sold, or

(iii) Offering some prizes to the buyers by the conduct of any contest, lottery or game of chance or skill, with real intention to promote sales or business.

4. **Non-compliance of Prescribed Standards:** Any sale or supply of goods, for use by consumers, knowing or having reason to believe that the goods do not comply with the standards prescribed by some competent authority, in relation to their performance, composition, contents, design construction, finishing or packing, as are necessary to prevent or reduce the risk of injury to the person using such goods, shall amount to an unfair trade practice.

5. **Hoarding, Destruction, etc.:** Any practice that permits the hoarding or destruction of goods, or refusal to sell the goods or provide any services, with an intention to raise the cost of those or other similar goods or services, shall be an unfair trade practice.

6. **Inquiry into Unfair Trade Practices:** The Commission may inquire into any unfair trade practice:

(i) Upon receiving a complaint from any trade association, consumer or a registered consumer association, or

(ii) Upon reference made to it by the Central Government or State Government, or

(iii) Upon an application to it by the Director General, or

(iv) Upon its own knowledge or information.

7. **Relief Available:** After making an inquiry into the unfair trade practice if the Commission is of the opinion that the practice is prejudicial to the public interest, or to the interest of any consumer it may direct that:

   (i) The practice shall be discontinued or shall not be repeated;

   (ii) The agreement relating thereto shall be void in respect of such unfair trade practice or shall stand modified;

   (iii) Any information, statement or advertisement relating to such unfair trade practice shall be disclosed, issued or published as may be specified;

   (iv) The Commission may permit the party to carry on any trade practice to take steps to ensure that it is no longer prejudicial to the public interest or to the interest of the consumer.

   However, no order shall be made in respect a trade practice which is expressly authorized by any law in force.

   The Commission is empowered to direct publication of corrective advertisement and disclosure of additional information while passing orders relating to unfair trade practices.

Monopolistic Trade Practices

A monopolistic trade practice is one, which has or is likely to have the effect of:

1. maintaining the prices of goods or charges for the services at an unreasonable level by limiting, reducing or otherwise controlling the production, supply or distribution of goods or services;

2. unreasonably preventing or lessening competition in the production, supply or distribution of any goods or services whether or not by adopting unfair method or fair or deceptive practices;
3. limiting technical development or capital investment to the common detriment;
4. deteriorating the quality of any goods produced, supplied or distributed; and
5. increasing unreasonably–
   (i) the cost of production of any good; or
   (ii) charges for the provision, or maintenance, of any services; or
   (iii) the prices for sale or resale of goods; or
   (iv) the profits derived from the production, supply or distribution of any goods or services.

A monopolistic trade practice is deemed to be prejudicial to the public interest, unless it is expressly authorized under any law or the Central Government permits to carry on any such practice.

Inquiry into Monopolistic Trade Practices

The Commission may inquire into any monopolistic trade practice,

1. Upon a reference made to it by the Central Government or
2. Upon an application made to it by the Director General or
3. Upon it own knowledge or information.

Relief Available

1. Where the inquiry by the Commission reveals that the trade practice inquired into operates or is likely to operate against public interest, the Central Government may pass such orders as it thinks fit to remedy or present any mischief resulting from such trade practice.
2. On an inquiry report of the Commission, the Central Government may—

(i) Prohibit the owner(s) of the concerned undertaking(s) from continuing to indulge in a monopolistic trade practice; or

(ii) Prohibit the owner of any class of undertakings or undertakings generally, from continuing to indulge in any monopolistic trade practice in relation to the goods or services.

3. The Central Government may also make an order:

(i) Regulating the production, storage, supply, distribution, or control of any goods or services by an undertaking and fixing the terms of their sale (including prices) or supply;

(ii) Prohibit any act or practice or commercial policy which prevents or lessens competition in the production, storage, supply or distribution of any goods or services;

(iii) Fixing standards for the goods used or produced by an undertaking;

(iv) Declaring unlawful the making or carrying out of the specified agreement;

(v) Requiring any party to the specified agreement to determine the agreement within the specified time, either wholly or to specified extent;

(vi) Regulating the profits which may be derived from the production, storage, supply, distribution or control of any goods or services; or

(vii) Regulating the quality of any goods or services so that their standard does not deteriorate.

Powers of the MRTP Commission

The MRTP Commission has the following powers:

1. Power of Civil Court under the Code of Civil Procedure, with respect to:

(i) Summoning and enforcing the attendance of any witness and examining him on oath;

(ii) Discovery and production of any document or other material object producible as evidence;

(iii) Reception of evidence on affidavits;

(iv) Requisition of any public record from any court or office;

(v) Issuing any commission for examination of witness; and

(vi) Appearance of parties and consequence of non-appearance.

2. Proceedings before the Commission are deemed as judicial proceedings within the meaning of Sections 193 and 228 of the Indian Penal Code.
3. To require any person to produce before it and to examine and keep any books of accounts or other documents relating to the trade practice, in its custody.
4. To require any person to furnish such information in respect of the trade practice as may be required or such other information as may be in his possession in relation to the trade carried on by any other person.
5. To authorize any of its officers to enter and search any undertaking or seize any books or papers, relating to an undertaking, in relation to which the inquiry is being made, if the Commission suspects that such books or papers are being or may be destroyed, mutilated, altered, falsified or secreted.

Remedies under the MRTP Act

The remedies available under this Act are—

Temporary Injunction

Where, during any inquiry, the Commission is satisfied that any undertaking or any person is carrying on, or is about to carry on, any monopolistic, restrictive or unfair trade practice, which is a pre-judicial to the public interest or the interest of any trader or class of traders generally, or of any consumer or class of consumers, or consumers generally, the Commission may grant a temporary injunction restraining such undertaking or person from carrying on such practice until the conclusion of inquiry or until further orders.

Compensation

Where any monopolistic, restrictive or unfair trade practice has caused damage to any Government, or trader or consumer, an application may be made to the Commission asking for compensation, and the Commission may award appropriate compensation.

Where any such loss or damage is caused to a number of persons having the same interest, compensation can be claimed with the permission of the Commission, by any of them on behalf of all of them.

FERA 1973 AND FEMA 1999

As a developing country which has been planning to quicken the process of its economic growth, India always wanted to use its foreign exchange wisely and judiciously. Even during the British rule, the government legislated measures to control foreign exchange under Defense of India Rules in 1939. The Indian government of free India used legislative provisions of foreign exchange control by enacting Imports and Exports (Control) Act, 1947. The amendments of the Act were made in 1957 and 1965. FERA was enacted in 1973.

In India, Foreign trade was regulated by: (a) The Foreign Trade (Development and Regulation) Act, 1992 which replaced the Imports and Exports (Control) Act, 1947 and (b) Foreign Exchange Regulations Act 1973. With the liberalization and globalization, the outlook changed. Now, it is the question of management and not regulation. However, certain activities are still being regulated in the interest of sovereignty of the nation.

FEMA Act 1999 came in the backdrop of the stringent regulatory provisions of FERA which were described as draconian and obnoxious in the wake of economic liberalization. FERA served the country to tide over the foreign exchange crisis and the controlled economic regime. Then, conservation and proper utilization of foreign exchange was the motto. FEMA came into effect from January 1, 2000 extends to the whole of India and applies to all branches, offices, and agencies outside India, owned or controlled by a person resident in India.

Objectives of FEMA Include

(i) facilitating external trade and payments and

(ii) promoting the orderly development and maintenance of foreign exchange market. FEMA deals with both current account and capital account transactions of the BOP.

In other words, the objectives of FEMA is to consolidate and amend FERA so as to promote foreign trade, while promoting the country's foreign exchange market.

Section 3 of the FEMA imposes restrictions on dealings in foreign exchange and foreign securities and payments to and receipts from any person outside India. The Act provides certain conditions.

FERA and FERA Compared

FERA is regulatory in nature; preventing misuse. It is a lengthy Act with 81 sections. Stipulations were rigid which included imprisonment. Many conditions were imposed in the export/import, blocked accounts and movement of human resources. FEMA is smaller enactment with 49 sections and facilitates trade and payments, and flow of exchange. Rigidity is removed in this Act compared to FERA. Only penalty is imposed and no imprisonment. Now, the conditions are highly liberal and provides a congenial climate for export/import of goods, services, human capital etc.

Salient Features

The prominent features of FEMA include:

- According to Section 3 of the FEMA 1999, no one shall deal in or transfer foreign exchange or foreign security to any unauthorized person. All receipts and payments shall be through authorized persons. RBI decides and approves the authorized dealers (AD). All banks dealing in foreign exchange are ADs.

- Section 4 of FEMA states that no Indian national shall acquire, hold, own, transfer any foreign exchange, foreign security or any immovable property located outside India except as otherwise provided for in the Act.
- Section 5 of FEMA provides that any person may sell or draw foreign exchange to or from an authorized person if such sale or drawal is one of current account transaction provided that the Central Government may, in public interest and in consultation with RBI, impose such reasonable restrictions for current account transactions, as may be prescribed.
- Section 5 of FEMA provides that any individual may sell or draw foreign exchange to or from any authorized person for capital account transaction. The RBI may in consultation with the Government of India specify the clause of permissible capital account transactions, the limits up to which foreign exchange be permissible for such transactions.
- Sub-section 4 of Section 6 stipulates that a person resident in India may hold, own, transfer or invest in foreign currency, foreign security or any immovable property located outside India, if such currency, security or property was acquired, held or owned by such person when he was resident outside India or inherited from a person who is resident outside India.
- Sub-section 5 of Section 6 of the Act applies to persons who reside outside India, i.e., they may hold, own transfer or invest in Indian currency, security or any immovable property situated in India if such currency, security or property was acquired, held or owned by such person when he was resident in India.
- Under Sub-section 6 of Section 6, the RBI is empowered by regulation of the said Act, to prohibit, restrict, or regulate establishment in India or a branch, office or other place of business by a person resident outside India, for the purpose of carrying on any activity relating to such branch, office or other place of business.

- Under FEMA, every exporter of goods shall declare to RBI a document containing true and correct material particulars including the amount representing the full export value of the goods exported without any delay for the purpose of ensuring the realization of the full export proceeds by such exporter. Moreover, every exporter of services shall declare to RBI a statement containing the true and correct material particulars in relation to payment for such services.
- Where any amount of foreign exchange is due or has accrued to any person resident in India, such person shall take all reasonable steps to realize and repatriate the amount to India within the time limit and manner specified by RBI.
- Current Account Transactions: Any person may sell or draw any foreign exchange to or from an authorized person if such sale or drawal is a current account transaction. As of now, all current account transactions are free subject to reasonable restrictions by Central Government in consultation with RBI (in public interest). Central Government has made Foreign Exchange Management (Current Account) Transactions Rules, 2000 which provides for prohibitions. Current account transactions are free subject to the above rules amended from time to time.
- Current Account Transactions: Prohibited List: Certain remittances are prohibited even if they are current account transactions. Transactions with Nepal/Bhutan: (a) Drawal of Foreign Exchange for travel to Nepal or Bhutan not permitted; (b) Transaction with a resident in Nepal or Bhutan cannot be made in foreign currency except when permitted by RBI.
- Current Account Transactions: Prior Approval of Government: The following transactions require prior approval of the Central Government:
  - Cultural tours
  - Advertisement by public sector undertakings/ Governments chartered vessel by public sector undertaking/Government payment of import on CIF

basis by public sector undertaking/Government through ocean transport agents of multi-modal transport

- Hire charges of Transponders Container detention charges beyond prescribed limits
- Prize money for sports
- Release of Foreign Exchange exceeding USD 10000 or its equivalent in a calendar year for one more private visits abroad (other than Nepal and Bhutan)
- Release of F/X exceeding USD 25000 or its equivalent in a calendar year for business travel, attending conference and specialized training
- Release of F/X exceeding USD 1 lakh or its equivalent for persons going abroad for employment
- Gift remittance to family members and relatives exceeding USD 5000 of its equivalent per remitter/donor per annum
- Donations exceeding USD 5000 or its equivalent per remitter/donor per annum.

- If any body contravenes any provision of FEMA, or contravenes any rule, regulation, notification, direction or order issued in exercise of the powers under this Act or contravenes any condition subject to which authorization is issued by RBI, such person shall be liable to penalty up to twice the sum involved in such contravention.
- If any body does not make full payment of the penalty awarded to him within 90 days of the notice issued to him in this context, he shall be liable for civil imprisonment.
- Section 40 of the Act empowers the Central Government to suspend or relax, either for a specific period or indefinitely, the operation of all or any of the provisions of FEMA. The notification, thus, issued by the Central Government will have to be approved by Parliament within a specified period.

- The Director of Enforcement shall investigate to prevent leakage of foreign exchange which generally occurs through certain malpractices.
- For enforcing the provisions of various sections of FEMA, the officers of Enforcement Directorate of the level of Assistant Director and above will have to undertake certain functions.
- The Deputy Director of Enforcement and officers of higher ranks investigate cases of contravention of the provisions of the Act. These proceedings are quasi-judicial in nature and commence with the issuance of show cause notice.
- Section 49 of the FEMA stipulates that no court can take cognizance of an offence under the repealed FERA and no adjudicating authority can take notice of any contravention under Section 51 of the repealed FERA after expiry of 2 years from the date of commencement of the FEMA.

SOCIO-CULTURAL AND THEIR IMPACT ON BUSINESS OPERATIONS

The term "socio-cultural environment" is typically used in business or marketing to describe an environment composed of forces and institutions impacting societal preferences, values and behaviours. Socio-cultural environment is a collection of social factors affecting a business and includes social traditions, values and beliefs, level of literacy and education, the ethical standards and State of society, the extent of social stratification, conflict and cohesiveness, and so forth. Socio-cultural environment consists of factors related to human relationships and the impact of social attitudes and cultural values on the business of the organization. The beliefs, values and norms of a society determine how individuals and organizations should be interrelated.

The core beliefs of a particular society tend to be rigid. It is difficult for businesses to change these core values, which become a determinant of its functioning. Some of the important factors and influences operating in this environment are as follows:

(a) Social concerns, such as the role of business in society, environmental pollution, corruption, use of mass media, and consumerism.

(b) Social attitudes and values, such as expectations of society from business, social customs, beliefs, rituals and practices, changing lifestyle patterns, and materialism.

(c) Family structure and the changes in it, attitude towards and within the family, and family values.

(d) Role of women in society, position of children and adolescents in family and society.

(e) Educational levels, awareness and consciousness of rights, and work ethics of members of society.

The social environment describes the people, their attitudes, social behaviour and impact of education, knowledge explosion and public opinion whereas cultural environment deals with values, norms and accepted behavioural patterns. The business must adjust its methods of operations with changing socio-cultural values. A person's relationship with the society he lives in shapes, refines and even alters his beliefs, values and norms which in turn define his tastes and preferences and even prompts him to absorb a world view of things. The process defines his relationship to his own self and others in the society, institutions, nature of the society and to the universe itself. In a social group, cultures and subcultures intermingle and some times tend to lose their uniqueness and individuality. In India, for instance, there are six major religions more than 1600 languages, all of which have some impact or the other on people living in the respective region. Regional differences in religion, language, customs, habits, values and social and caste systems are a legion and make India's socio-cultural environment both unique and complex. The socio-cultural environment shapes the attitudes of human beings, though there may be great diversity in its impact.

The human problem in society is how people behave and what attitudes they have towards the role of their fellowmen and their society. Even the most brilliant, and well educated man might turn to be an unproductive employee if he does not bring his brilliance and education to the work he does, but instead dislikes his boss, thinks his company is exploiting him, and he has a dim future. There may be others who may not be so well-endowed, but may be discharging their duties better because of their genial attitude towards their fellow human beings. So, in this context, it must be stressed that what is needed is right social attitude.

Culture is the collective programming of the mind that distinguishes the members of one category of people from those of another. Different global consumer cultures are emerging.

Socio-cultural factors influence the consumption pattern which has a direct bearing on business. The lifestyle, openness to new thinks influence the business what to produce and how to shape the product. The mind set of the entrepreneur influences the investment decision by the businessman. A conservative entrepreneur may not like to expand business beyond his necessities which restricts business growth. Hence, the socio-cultural aspects influence and impact business.

CHECK YOUR UNDERSTATING

1. Describe political-legal culture.
2. What ate the important provisions of the Indian Constitution pertaining to business?
3. What are the prominent features of MRTP and Competition Law? What is the role played by each of these regulations?
4. What are important features of FERA and how FEMA distinguishes from earlier regulations?
5. How socio-cultural environment impacts business operations?
6. Explain the meaning, relevance and features of the Competition Act, 2002.

REFERENCES

1. Fernando, A.C.: Business Environment, Pearson Education, New Delhi.
2. Raj, Rituparna: A Study in Business Ethics, Himalaya Publishing House Pvt. Ltd., Mumbai, 1999.
3. Tata Services Ltd.: Statistical Outline of India 2008-2009. Tata Services Ltd., 2009.
4. Bhat Govinda K. Dr., Ayodya Sumita: Business Ethics and Corporate Social Responsibility, Himalaya Publishing House Pvt. Ltd., Mumbai.

Chapter 5
Indian Culture and Values

This Chapter deals with:

- What is Culture?
- Importance of Culture in Human life
- Salient Features of Indian Culture and Values

INTRODUCTION

Before launching into the vast ocean of Indian Culture and making a bid for its salient features, it will be useful if we have a clear conception of what we mean by culture. The term 'culture' is perhaps the most widely used one in our day-to-day conversation. Generally, the arts, music, dance, sports and other entertainments which add joy to life pass under the name of national culture even to the exclusion of more important things which give definite and unique shape to the culture of a place.

WHAT IS CULTURE?

Culture refers to the patterns of thought and behaviour of people. It includes values, beliefs, rules of conduct, and patterns of social, political and economic organisation. These are passed on from one generation to the next by formal as well as informal processes. Culture consists of the ways in which we think and act as members of a society. Thus, all the achievements of group life are collectively called culture. In popular parlance, the material aspects of culture, such as scientific and technological achievements are seen as distinct from culture which is left with the non-material, higher achievements of group life (art, music, literature, philosophy, religion and science). Culture is the product of such an organization and expresses itself through language and art, philosophy and religion. It also expresses itself through social habits, customs, economic organizations and political institutions.

The English word "Culture" is derived from the Latin term "cult or cultus" meaning tilling, or cultivating or refining and worship. In sum, it means cultivating and refining a thing to such an extent that its end product evokes our admiration and respect. This is practically the same as "Sanskriti" of the Sanskrit language.

Culture is a way of life. The food you eat, the clothes you wear, the language you speak in and the God you worship all are aspects of culture. In very simple terms, we can say that culture is the embodiment of the way in which we think and do things. It is also the things that we have inherited as members of society. All the achievements of human beings as members of social groups can be called culture. Art, music, literature, architecture, sculpture, philosophy, religion and science can be seen as aspects of culture. However, culture also includes the customs, traditions, festivals, ways of living and one's outlook on various issues of life.

A civilized society living at a particular place often develops a way of life. This way of life, conditioned by its natural surroundings and its climate, is held in high regard by the members of the group and is transmitted to the next generation with all the additions made by the present one. The sum total of this way of life built up by the group for generations is called its culture.

"Culture, in the technical sense of social organization, is often defined as the complex of ideas, conceptions, developed qualities, and organized relationships and courtesies that exist generally in a society" says K.M. Panikkar. Prof. R. Firth includes under culture all learned behaviour which has been socially acquired.

In studying culture, we are concerned with ideas and values that are found in religious and moral codes, in literature, science, philosophy, art and music. According to C. Rajagopalachari, the culture of a people is what is desired and expected by the best among them actually to prevail and govern their daily life. It is an accepted predictable standard of conduct and deportment which the people strive to reach every day.

Culture in an individual expresses himself through overt actions and comes to notice more clearly than virtue. Character is the inside of a man; culture is external and has to do with behaviour, speech, conduct and the way of living. A cultured man is an embellishment to the society; he not only makes his life sweet but also delights others. Culture is a definite addition to personality.

IMPORTANCE OF CULTURE IN HUMAN LIFE

Culture is closely linked with life. It is not an add-on, an ornament that we as human beings can use. It is not merely a touch of colour. It is what makes us human. Without culture, there would be no humans. Culture is made up of traditions, beliefs, way of life, from the most spiritual to the most material. It gives us meaning, a way of leading our lives. Human beings are creators of culture and, at the same time, culture is what makes us human. A fundamental element of culture is the issue of religious belief and its symbolic expression. We must value religious identity and be aware of current efforts to make progress in terms of interfaith dialogue, which is actually an intercultural dialogue. As the world is becoming more and more global and we coexist on a more global level, we can't just think there's only one right way of living or that any one is valid. The need for coexistence makes the coexistence of cultures and beliefs necessary. In order to not make such mistakes, the best thing we can do is get to know other cultures, while also getting to know our own. How can we dialogue with other cultures, if we don't really know what our own culture is? The three eternal and universal values of Truth, Beauty and Goodness are closely linked with culture. It is culture that brings us closer to truth through philosophy and religion; it brings beauty in our lives through the arts and makes us aesthetic beings; and it is culture that makes us ethical beings by bringing us closer to other human beings and teaching us the values of love, tolerance and peace.

SALIENT FEATURES OF INDIAN CULTURE

The culture of India is the way of life of the people of India. India's languages, religions, dance, music, architecture, food, and customs differ from place to place within the country. The Indian culture, often labeled as an amalgamation of several cultures, spans across the Indian subcontinent and has been influenced by a history that is several millennia old. Many elements of India's diverse cultures, such as Indian religions, yoga and Indian cuisine, have had a profound impact across the world.

Great civilizations of the past—of Egypt, Babylon, Assyria and Persia—have disappeared from the face of the earth and only their sepulchers remain. But the civilization of India has lived through so many cataclysms throughout the centuries and in the midst of dire vicissitudes has preserved the thread of its continuity. And the reason is not far to seek. The former civilizations failed to develop a culture of their own and necessarily culture is less pervasive than the machinery of civilization. But the case of India is different. Here, culture is almost as pervasive as civilization itself.

Indian culture has often been misunderstood not only by her foreign critics but also by Indians trained in the Western tradition and blinded by a rationalistic bias. Very often, even the existence of such a thing as Indian culture has been denied. But the truth is otherwise. Though there is no need to defend our culture today, still, it is imperative that we should ourselves have a clear idea of what our ancestors had achieved for themselves and for humanity.

India has been the meeting place of conflicting races and civilizations. She has tried to achieve a unity out of the heterogeneous elements which make the totality of her life. She has a life-view of her own. This makes up her culture which extends over more than three thousand years and has found expression in her art and literature and philosophy.

Let us now make an attempt to analyze the salient features of Indian Culture which is so vast and varied and has such a long and continuous history.

Spirit of Tolerance

An important characteristic of Indian culture is its attitude of toleration which has fostered simultaneous development of different strands. Jews and Zoroastrians sought and found asylum in India. Christian colonies flourished here in second century A.D. Forty-five million followers of Islam live here in perfect peace and harmony. India has successfully upheld her tradition of religious and social toleration by her unending insistence on the peculiar character of the state.

Whenever Indian religion has been challenged from inside or from outside, it has met the challenge with an open mind. Buddha has been accepted as one of the avataras. The old texts of Hinduism were reinterpreted in the light of the impact of Islam in the 14th and 15th centuries and of Christianity in the 18th and 19th centuries. And this reinterpretation has given birth to vital movements of reform and put new vigour into the body of Hinduism. This spirit of tolerance is responsible for the richness and variety of Indian life and the complex pattern of Indian Culture.

Spirit of Synthesis

India's power of assimilation, too, has always been remarkable Her culture has flowed in one continuous process of gradual change and acceptance and assimilation of ideas totally different from its own.

When the Aryans came to India, they took much from the Dravidians and built their culture on its basis. This process has been a continuous one, and very epoch has made its contribution and all these contributions have been fused into an integral whole. Today, India represents a true meeting ground of East and West.

Respect for the Individual

Indian people have a firm faith in the belief that there is a connection between the individual soul – Jivatma – and the universal soul – Paramatma. This philosophical outlook has fostered a feeling of universal brotherhood which has expressed itself in tolerance and willingness to effect a synthesis of diverse influences. It has also engendered a deep respect for the individual.

Open Attitude to Science

Indian culture had an open attitude to science. Indian religion never preached a dogmatic view about the material aspects of the universe. The Indian mind never had a distrust of science and the ideas about the roundness of the earth and evolution, etc. found ready acceptance in India. A strong intellectuality marked the whole ancient spirit. "The mass of the intellectual production during the period from Asoka well into the Mohammedan epoch is something truly prodigious," said Sri Aurobindo. And this intellectual vitality has enabled us in the present day to catch up with the modern world without having to deny any essential aspect of our culture.

Harmony with Nature

Indian culture has sought to achieve harmony with nature. Mountains, rivers, trees, and flowers have a special significance for the Indian people who never had to carry a struggle for existence against the ruthlessness of nature.

Another distinguishing feature of Indian culture is its insistence on the unity of all Nature and community of living beings. This feeling of kinship with Nature has given birth to the doctrine of Ahimsa which is another name for tenderness for all living beings. The doctrine of reincarnation has reiterated belief in Ahimsa for we see the soul of our departed relations in the animals and insects and avoid cruelty to them.

Expression in Conduct and Norms of Behaviour

Culture is not a matter of mere ideas. It finds expression through conduct and behaviour in society. Almost all the cultures emphasise reverence towards elders and teachers, respect and affection towards relatives, courtesy towards strangers, honour towards womanhood and tenderness towards children. But in Indian culture, parents and gurus are recipients of special reverence.

The large joint family forms a special pattern of our culture. Here, every member has his place with its fixed rights and duties and an accepted code of conduct towards others. The Indian attitude towards womanhood has always been one of essential reverence. Worship of shakti in the form of Durga and Kali has had a large following in the country.

Marriage among the Indians is a family affair and an inviolable contract of partnership. Even death does not part the couple once they are tied together before the holy fire.

According to C. Rajagopalachari, "Indian culture is predominantly 'self-restraint': sharing your sustenance with the poor, chastity, the rigours of widowhood, austerity, sanyas, all-round religious tolerance—these forms and aspects of restraint make up Indian culture." Indian culture lays special emphasis on three cardinal virtues—dama, daana and daya which are different forms of self-restraint.

Rich Artistic Heritage

Art is the creative expression of great cultures and a significant characteristic of Indian culture is the world of beauty in music, literature, architecture and other arts which she has created as embodying her ideals.

Indian art is, in fact, identified in its spiritual aim and principle with the rest of Indian culture. The temples of Ellora, reliefs at Sanchi and Amravati and frescoes at Ajanta present a haunting world of beauty and are without parallel. Indian art tradition crossed the frontiers of India and spread to Java, Siam and Cambodia.

The greatness and glory of Indian music is being slowly recognized by the people of the world in the present day. Indian culture is deeply linked with Sanskrit literature whose importance as a whole consists in its originality. This vast literature embodies a noble civilization and is practically unsurpassed and unequalled in every field — epic, poetry, drama or lyrical expression.

Four Duties

Civilizations can be and are generally materialistic, but there is no culture which is not essentially spiritual. The pre-eminence of Hinduism in India gives to Indian culture its special characteristics. Indian culture has undoubtedly a religious background like all other cultures, still it is not a religious culture, but an essentially secular one.

Indian culture made spiritual truth the grand uplifting idea of life, the core of all thinking, the foundation of all religions, the secret sense and declared ultimate aim of human existence.

Indian culture has succeeded in stamping spiritual truths on the earthly life through its insistence on two conceptions of Purusharthas and the ashramas, which lie at the root of the Indian way of life. The Purusharthas or the objectives of our life on this earth are Dharma, Artha, Kaama, and Moksha. Dharma here means the fundamental moral law governing the functioning of the universe. It is just another name for insistence on high moral life. Artha covers productive and gainful occupations and the promotion of social welfare. Kaama is not only desire or lust, it signifies physical and artistic enjoyment, the life of the senses in the broadest sense. Poetry, drama, song, dance, music, etc. were all made instruments of the culture of the spirit.

The aim of the social system was a harmony of Artha, Kaama and Dharma, and this self-perfecting process raised the life of the individual beyond this level to the supernal height of spiritual freedom, Moksha. Moksha completes the picture and was to be attained as a result of a full life of Dharma, Artha and Kaama. And, for this, the individual was provided a framework, a gradation, for his life. Individual life was divided into four successive stages, called the Aashramas: the life of the student, acquiring knowledge, developing self-discipline and self-control and continence; the life of the house-holder; the life of the recluse or the elder statesman, who had attained a certain poise and objectivity, and could devote himself to public work without the selfish desire to profit by it; and lastly the life of the super-social man who lived a life largely cut off from the world's activities. Through these stages, "they adjusted the two opposing tendencies which often exist side by side in man—the acceptance of life in its fullness, and the rejection of it" – Jawaharlal Nehru.

What has been stated in the foregoing paragraphs may be summarized as follows in the eloquent language of Sri Aurobindo: "So founded, so trained, the ancient Indian race grew to astounding heights of culture and civilization, lived with a noble well-founded, ample and vigorous order and freedom, developed a great literature, sciences, arts, crafts, industries, rose to high ideals of knowledge and culture, arduous greatness and heroism... discovered the profoundest truths of self and the world."

A Cosmic Vision

The framework of Indian culture places human beings within a conception of the universe as a divine creation. It is not anthropo-centric (human-centric) only and considers all elements of creation, both living and non-living, as manifestations of the divine. Therefore, it respects God's design and promotes the ideal of co-existence. This vision, thus, synthesizes human beings, nature and God into one integral whole. This is reflected in the idea of satyam-shivam-sundaram.

Sense of Harmony

Indian philosophy and culture tries to achieve an innate harmony and order and this is extended to the entire cosmos. Indian culture assumes that natural cosmic order inherent in nature is the foundation of moral and social order. Inner harmony is supposed to be the foundation of outer harmony. External order and beauty will naturally follow from inner harmony. Indian culture balances and seeks to synthesize the material and the spiritual, as aptly illustrated by the concept of Purushartha.

Adaptability

Adaptability has a great contribution in making Indian culture immortal. Adaptability is the process of changing according to time, place and period. It is an essential element of longevity of any culture. Indian culture has a unique property of adjustment, as a result of which, it is maintained till today. Indian family, caste, religion and institutions have changed themselves with time. Due to adaptability and co-ordination of Indian culture, its continuity, utility and activity is still present.

Dr. Radha Krishnan, in his book, *'Indian Culture: Some Thoughts'*, while describing the adaptability of Indian culture has said all people whether black or white, Hindus or Muslims, Christians or Jews are brothers and our country is the entire universe. We should have devotion for those things, which are beyond the limits of knowledge and regarding which, it's difficult to say anything. Our hope towards mankind was based on that respect and devotion, which people had towards other's views. There should be no efforts on imposing our thoughts on others.

Receptivity

Receptivity is an important characteristic of Indian culture. Indian culture has always accepted the good of the invading cultures. Indian culture is like an ocean, in which many rivers come and meet. In the same way, all castes succumbed to the Indian culture and very rapidly they dissolved in the Hindutva. Indian culture has always adjusted with other cultures it's ability to maintain unity amongst the diversities of all is the best. The reliability, which developed in this culture due to this receptivity, is a boon for this world and is appreciated by all. We have always adopted the properties of various cultures. Vasudaiva Kutumbakam is the soul of Indian culture.

Indian culture has always answered and activated itself by receiving and adjusting with the elements of foreign cultures. Indian culture has received the elements of Muslim cultures and has never hesitated in accepting the useful things of foreign culture. Therefore, its continuity, utility and activity are still there today. The adaptability and receptivity of this culture has given it the power to remain alive in all the conditions. Due to this property, Indian culture was never destroyed even after facing the foreign attacks. Actually, Indian society and culture had facilitated foreign attackers by getting them close and becoming intimate with them and not only gave but also received many things

Spirituality

Spirituality is the soul of Indian culture. Here, the existence of soul is accepted. Therefore, the ultimate aim of man is not physical comforts but is self-realization. Radha Kumud Mukerjee, in his book, *'Hindu Civilization'*, has analyzed that Indian culture, which kept its personal specialities, bound the entire nation in unity in such a way that nation and culture were considered inseparable and became unanimous. Nation became culture and culture became nation. Country took the form of Spiritual World, beyond the physical world. When Indian culture originated in the times of Rigveda, then it spread with time to Saptasindhu, Bramhavarta, Aryavarta, Jumbudweepa, Bharata Varsha or India. Because of its strength, it reached abroad beyond the borders of India and established there also.

Thoughts about Karma and Reincarnation

The concept of Karma (action) and Reincarnation have special importance in Indian culture. It is believed that one gains virtue during good action and takes birth in higher order in his next birth and spends a comfortable life. The one doing bad action takes birth in lower order in his next birth and suffers pain and leads a miserable life. Upanishads say that the principle of fruits of action is correct.

A man gets the fruits as per the action he does. Therefore, man needs to modify his actions, so as to improve the next birth also. Continuously performing good actions in all his birth, he will get salvation, i.e., will be liberated from the cycle of birth and death. This concept is not only of the Upanishads but is also the basis of the Jainism, Buddhism, etc. In this way, the concept of reincarnation is associated with the principle of action. The actual cause of reincarnation is the actions done in the previous birth.

Emphasis on Duty

As against rights, Indian culture emphasises dharma or moral duty. It is believed that performance of one's duty is more important than asserting one's right. It also emphasizes the complementariness between one's own duty and other's rights. Thus, through the emphasis on community or family obligations, Indian culture promotes interdependence rather than Independence and autonomy of the individual.

Unity in Diversity

An important characteristic of Indian culture is Unity in Diversity. There is much diversity in Indian culture like in geography, in caste, in creed, in language, in religion, in politics, etc. Dr. R.K.Mukerjee writes, "India is a museum of different types, communities, customs, traditions, religions, cultures, beliefs, languages, castes and social system But even after having so much of external diversity, none can deny the internal unity of Indian culture". Thus, in Indian culture, there is Unity in Diversity. According to Pandit Nehru, "Those who see India, are deeply moved by its Unity in Diversity. No one can break this unity". This fundamental unity of India is its great fundament element.

According to Sir Herbert Rizle, "Even after the linguistic, social and geographical diversity, a special uniformity is seen from Kanyakumari to the Himalayas. Indian culture is a huge tree, the roots of which have Aryan culture. Like a new layer is formed all around the tree every year, similarly layers of many historical eras surround the tree of Indian culture, protecting it and getting life sap from it. We all live in the cooling shade of that tree". The concept of Unity and diversity will be dealt in details in separate paragraphs.

CHECK YOUR UNDERSTANDING

1. Discuss different aspects of Indian culture.
2. Discuss the concept of Unity and diversity in Indian culture.
3. Explain the salient features of traditional Indian culture.
4. How will you define the concept of culture?

5. What are the general characteristics of culture?
6. What is culture? Discuss it.

REFERENCES

1. Gore, M.S.: Unity in Diversity: The Indian Experience in Nation-building, Rawat Publication, Jaipur, 2002.
2. Kabir, Humayun: Our Heritage, National Information and Publications Ltd., Mumbai, 1946.
3. Malik, S.C.: Understanding Indian Civilization: A Framework of Enquiry, Indian Institute of Advanced Study, Simla, 1975.
4. Mukerji, D.P.: Sociology of Indian Culture, Rawat Publications, Jaipur, 1948/1979.
5. Pandey, Govind Chandra: Foundations of Indian Culture, Books and Books, New Delhi, 1984.

Chapter 6: Environmental Ethics

This Chapter deals with:

- Economic Environment
- Economic Growth and its Implications for Business
- Economic Planning and its Implications on Business
- Industrial Policy and Government Control over Business
- Role of FICCI and CII

INTRODUCTION

Environmental ethics concerns human beings' moral relationship with the natural environment. It seeks to help people and their leaders to act responsibly when they do things that impact the natural world.

The emergence of the field of environmental ethics was due to the increasing awareness in the 1960s of the effects that technology, industry, economic expansion, and population growth were having on the environment. It is all the more relevant today as most environmental problems are the result of the unethical actions of individuals or organizations. For example, water quality degradation in the Yamuna river where some polluting sources are discharging polluted effluent in drains joining the river. In Mumbai, the Mithi river receives domestic wastewater from areas like Sakinaka to Kurla, Chunabhatti and Mahim.

As population continue to increase, the various problems caused by too many people naturally increase in both their number and seriousness. Of course, pollution and the depletion of natural resources are not only environmental concerns but dwindling plant and animal biodiversity, the loss of wilderness, the degradation of ecosystems, and climate change are all part of a raft of "green" issues that have implanted themselves into both public consciousness and public policy over subsequent years. There are many ethical decisions that human beings make with respect to the environment. For example:

- Should we continue to cut forests for the sake of human consumption?
- Should we continue to make petrol and diesel powered vehicles, depleting fossil fuel resources while the technology exists to create zero emission vehicles?
- Destruction of Ozone layer due to the human-created chemicals?
- What environmental obligations do we need to keep for future generations?
- Is it right for humans to knowingly cause the extinction of a species for the convenience of humanity?

BUSINESS ENVIRONMENT DEFINED

Business environment is the sum total of all external and internal factors that influence a business. You should keep in mind that external factors and internal factors can influence each other and work together to affect a business. For example, a health and safety regulation is an external factor that influences the internal environment of business operations. Additionally, some external factors are beyond your control. These factors are often called external constraints. Let's take a look at some key environmental factors.

Business environment is so powerful that it can make economic development. It can create employment opportunities and can pave a way for the rich society. In the absence of a suitable environment, unemployment, poverty, economic destruction etc. are to be faced by a country. Only after evaluating the changing environment, and making forecasts for the future, a business should formulate its policies and should formulate plans for future.

ECONOMIC ENVIRONMENT

The economic environment consists of external factors in a business market and the broader economy that can influence a business. You can divide the economic environment into the microeconomic environment, which affects business decision-making – such as individual actions of firms and consumers – and the macroeconomic environment, which affects an entire economy and all of its participants. Many economic factors act as external constraints on your business, which means that you have little, if any, control over them. Let's take a look at both of these broad factors in more detail.

External environment largely consists of uncontrollable factors which influence a firm's action and direction, organizational structure and internal processes. This environment can be divided into two interrelated categories: (i) those in remote environment and (ii) those in more immediate operating environment. Some authors refer remote environment as macro environment and operating environment as micro environment or task or competitive environment.

Business is a microeconomic unit. The market behaviour of a firm depicts the economic decisions of a firm. Economic environment refers to all those economic factors which have a bearing on the functioning of a business unit. The importance of economic environment can be understood by the fact that more and more economist are finding place in industrial establishments.

The economic environment of a business is complex in nature. The different sectors together influence the trends and structure of economy and a business firm has economic relations with these sectors, viz., government, capital market, foreign sectors and household sector. Economic environment of a country includes there main elements. These are: (i) economic system, (ii) economic policies and (iii) economic conditions.

Economic System

The economic system of a country reflects the economic composition, economic thinking and economic liberalization. The economic system may be of three types – socialist, capitalist and mixed. The study of these systems helps in understanding about a country's stand. It also helps in preparation of the business strategies. The detailed discussion of all of these is as follows:

(a) Socialist Economic System: Under socialistic economic system, the factors of production are to be organized, owned and managed by the government. The benefits of this goes to the public. In socialistic system, efforts are made to provide employment to all and gives suitable rewards to each worker for the efforts put in by him. The communalist countries like Russia, China, Czechoslovakia, East Germany, Hungary, Poland, etc. have centrally planned economies. The State would own and direct all instruments of production. Sharing in the distributive process would have no relationship to private property since this right would not exist. The world socialism and capitalism are interchangeable. Main characteristics of the socialistic pattern of economies are as follows:

- Government control and ownership
- Role and interference of Government
- Planning by Government
- Emphasis on equality of income
- Price and wage control by Government
- Lack of free competition
- No complete freedom of business, profession, employment etc.

(b) Capitalist Economic Systems: A capitalist economic system is that system which encourages private enterprises, free play of market forces, strong competition and directs the scarce resources to most profitable ones. The freedom of private initiative is the greatest in capitalist economy, which is characterized by the following assumptions:

- The factors of production (labour, land and capital) are privately owned, and production occurs at the initiative of private enterprise.
- Income is received in monetary form by the sale of services of the factors of production and form the profits of the private enterprise.
- Members of the free market economy have freedom of choice insofar as consumption, occupation, savings and investment are concerned.
- The free market economy is not planned, controlled or regulated by the Government.

The results of capitalist economy are drastic one, viz., inequality of income, exploitation of poor, corruption and recurrence of trade cycle. The wasteful expenditure on luxuries and consumer durables increases in the capitalist economy due to increased income of a section of people.

(c) Mixed Economy: It is a midway between socialist economy and capitalist economy. Co-existence of both public and private sectors is the feature of mixed economy. Our Indian economy system is also a mixed economic system. Public sector is managed and controlled by the State. But for the control of private sector also, State formulates different rules and regulations. Generally, the public sector companies are established by the State which are strategic and have national importance. The mixed economic system can be divided into three parts:

- The enterprises wholly owned and controlled by State
- The enterprises jointly owned by State and private entrepreneurs
- The enterprises wholly owned and controlled by private entrepreneurs under the general control and regulation of the State.

The main characteristics of *Mixed Economy* are as follows:

- Centralized planning
- Government control over policies, preferences and resource allotment
- Public distribution channel under the supervision of Government
- Control of Government over economic activities through monetary and fiscal policies
- Co-existence of public, private and joint sector
- Freedom of selection of profession, employment and trade
- Freedom of saving and investment
- Uncontrolled consumption pattern

ECONOMIC POLICIES

The term economic policy refers to Government policy towards economy as a whole. These policies have great impact on the business. Economic policy establishes relationship between Government and business. The effect of these policies may be favourable for some categories of business, unfavourable for some other categories or neutral in respect of others. For example, an industry may get the nod of priority sector and may be awarded with incentives or subsidies while the other industry may face hard decisions due to wastage of resources by them. Similarly, with the objective of equal distribution and planned industrial growth, the establishment of industry in the backward region may be subsidized, while establishment of industry in advanced or developed region may face strict government regulations.

In India, government regulatory factors are considerably more significant than other environmental factors. Indeed, reflecting the government's far-reaching intervention in and overhauling of market forces, there is a plethora of regulations, both positive and negative, which have explicit as well as implicit bearing on the prospects of business and industry in India. These include:

- Industrial policy
- Fiscal policy
- Tax policy
- Rationing and price control in specific and product markets
- Public expenditure policy
- Public debt policy
- Foreign Exchange Regulation Act
- Regulation of priority sector credit
- Import-export policy
- Industrial licensing policy
- Monopolies and Restrictive Trade Policies Act 1969 (MRTPA) for control over expansion of existing capacity and creation of fresh capacity
- Distribution control through State Trading and Public Distribution Agencies
- Income, employment and price policy

Changes in these policies have its impact on the business community. For example, in order to promote export of gold jewellery, the number of nominated agencies has been increased for stocking gold, whereas in past, it is being done only by MMTC, STC, SBI and HHEC. Government decision to extend fiscal protection and incentive to powerloom sector had serious impact on the textile mills.

ECONOMIC CONDITIONS

The impact of economic environmental changes can be seen in business prospects over time in different ways. Increase in Green Revolution in certain parts of India lead to growth in demand for a number of products like transistors, radio sets, bicycles, tubewells and low horsepower motors as well as synthetic textiles. Improvement in economic conditions improved the styles and quality of living and purchasing power of the public. The consumption level, economic position of public, level of living, etc. have great impact on the business as the growth and expansion, innovations, new models, new types of products, etc. depends on the demand of the public.

The economic conditions include the following:

- Capital formation
- Industrial development of a country
- Economic structure of a country
- Business organization structure
- Entrepreneurship
- Consumption level
- Size of market
- Supply of natural resources
- Human resource
- Foreign capital
- Foreign trade
- Innovations
- Rate of interest and banking system
- Price index
- Welfare schemes in the country.

In countries where income levels are high, business conditions are prosperous. In the developing countries like India, where purchasing power of the people is not so good, business have to reduce the price or lower the quality of the product.

WHY THE ECONOMIC ENVIRONMENT IS IMPORTANT?

The economic environment of business will play a pivotal role in determining the success or failure of a business.

Let's first consider some macroeconomic factors. If interest rates are too high, the cost of borrowing may not permit a business to expand. On the other hand, if unemployment rate is high, businesses can obtain labour at cheaper costs. However, if unemployment is too high, this may result in a recession and less discretionary consumer spending resulting in insufficient sales to keep the business going. Tax rates will take a chunk of your income and currency exchange rates can either help or hurt the exporting of the products to specific foreign markets.

Now let's turn our attention to microeconomic factors for a bit. Market size may determine the viability of entering into a new market. If a market is too small, there may not be sufficient demand and profit potential. This leads us to the concept of demand and supply. If the product is in high demand but there is a low supply of it, the business unit is going to make a tidy profit, but if the product is in low demand and the market is flooded with similar products, business may face bankruptcy. The quality and quantity of the competition will affect how well business is winning customers in the marketplace. Suppliers are the arteries pumping vital supplies and resources for production. If there are problems with suppliers, it can clog up those arteries and cause serious problems. Likewise, the type of relationship with your distributors, such as retail stores, may influence how quickly the products leave their shelves.

ECONOMIC GROWTH AND BUSINESS

Economic growth is important if businesses are to grow and prosper. It relates to growth in the output of the economy as a whole. Growth is measured as the change in the gross domestic product (GDP) of a country over one year. For comparisons over time, this figure must be adjusted to allow for inflation and the resulting value is called 'real growth'. Over time, real economic growth leads to major improvements in living standards, expanding existing markets and opening new ones. The real economic growth of one country relative to another is an important indicator of business opportunity.

ECONOMIC PLANNING

Economic planning is a mechanism for economic co-ordination contrasted with the market mechanism. There are various types of planning procedures and ways of conducting economic planning. As a co-ordinating mechanism for socialism and an alternative to the market, planning is defined as a direct allocation of resources and is contrasted with the indirect allocation of the market.

The level of centralization in decision-making in planning depends on the specific type of planning mechanism employed. As such, one can distinguish between *centralized* planning and *decentralized* planning. An economy primarily based on central planning is referred to as a planned economy. In a centrally planned economy, the allocation of resources is determined by a comprehensive plan of production which specifies output requirements. Planning may also take the form of *directive* planning or *indicative planning.* Most modern economies are mixed economies incorporating various degrees of markets and planning.

A distinction can be made between physical planning (as in pure socialism) and financial planning (as practiced by governments and private firms in capitalism). Physical planning involves economic planning and co-ordination conducted in terms of disaggregated physical units; whereas financial planning involves plans formulated in terms of financial units. Economic Planning helps in mobilizing and allocating the resources in desired manner. Objectives of economic planning is to reduce inequality, attain economic growth, balanced regional growth and modernization. Each five year plan aims at achieving certain target Five year plan constitutes the steps toward the fulfillment of objectives of economic planning.

The present is an era of economic planning. No country in the world can achieve rapid rate of economic growth on the basis of the economic activities undertaken by the private sector alone. It is necessary that government should actively participate in economic development with planned framework to achieve the rapid economic growth. Economic planning is a process under which attempts are made to achieve given targets of economic development within a specified period of time. Economic planning refers to that method under which a central planning authority keeping in view the resources of the country seeks to control the economic factors in order to achieve pre-determined objectives within a specified time. Both developed and underdeveloped countries have adopted planning but there is the difference between the two: it is corrective planning in the former and in the latter it is development planning.

Main Features of Economic Planning

Main features of economic planning are as under:

1. **Central Planning Authority:** Under economic planning, there is a Central Planning Authority appointed by the State. All central economic decisions like what to produce, how much to produce, for whom to produce and how to produce, are taken by it. This authority surveys physical and human resources of the country and formulates a comprehensive plan to achieve set objects. In India, this function is performed by Planning Commission.
2. **Democratic:** The first and the foremost feature of the Indian planning is that it is socially based and democratic in nature. Indian planning is called as democratic because the planning is done by the democratically elected government. In addition to this, opinions of various organizations, institutions, experts are being given with due considerations while formulating a plan. It may also be termed as socially oriented political planning because social factor is given more consideration than economic factor in the Indian plans. The impact of all those factors which affect political environment can also be seen in the plans.
3. **Indicative Economic Planning:** The Indian Government generally lays targets for the sectors which are external to the government control, i.e., agriculture. Indian agriculture is totally privatized and the Government has no control over it. But in Five Year Plans, it lays targets for the sector. Doubtlessly, the Government provides some facilities and incentives like, subsidy on fertilizers, seeds, support price, etc., to boost the sector. Still the management of agriculture and allied activities rests in private hands and therefore, the Government cannot be sure to achieve the laid targets.

4. **Decentralized Planning:** The need and importance of decentralized planning was emphasized since the application of the first five year plan. But planning remained centralized till the sixth five year plan. The seventh plan witnessed the decentralized planning for the first time in India. Decentralized planning is the delegation of planning activities, to the sub-state levels, i.e., district, sub-division, block and village level. In other words, decentralized planning starts from the grass root level. It emphasizes on the grass root planning, i.e., district planning, sub-division planning, block level planning and village level planning so that the needs of the society can be included in the plans.
5. **Regulatory Mechanism:** The Planning Commission of India plays the role of regulatory mechanism. It gives necessary direction and provides regulation over the planning system. In addition to this, a co-ordination agency, namely, the National Development Council (NDC) was set up in 1952 by the Government of India to co-ordinate between Centre and States. Presently, planning decisions, originate from Commission and are finally approved by the Council. The implementation of planning comes under the purview of Planning Commission.
   (a) **Basic Objectives:** Each and every plan has certain basic or fundamental objectives. These objectives are found to be common in most of our plans. The basic objective is the growth with social justice in the economic planning in India.
   (b) **Existence of Central Plan and State Plan:** In our five year plan, there is co-existence of both the Central Plan and State Plans. Separate outlays are made for both. Central plans are controlled by Planning Commission and the Central Government, whereas, the State Plan is under the exclusive control of State Planning Boards and State Governments. But the State Government has to seek approval from the Planning Commission.

(c) **Public Sector and Private Sector Plans:** Allocation of resources is made separately both for public sector and private sector. It is because of the reason that Indian economy is a mixed economy.

(d) **Balanced Regional Development:** Balanced regional development is emphasized in each five year plan. It is due to the reason that some regions are economically backward and it is felt necessary to give more weightage to them. These regions are given special category status, so that the additional resources may be channelized for their developments.

(e) **Definite Time:** Each plan is of definite time period. For instance, each plan in India is of five year period. One plan succeeds the other. Planning is a process.

Objectives of Planning

Main objectives of economic planning may be divided into economic objectives, social objectives and political objectives.

Economic objectives include:

1. Economic growth
2. Increase in National Income and Per Capita Income
3. Reduction of inequalities
4. Reduction in regional inequalities
5. Full employment
6. Rapid industrialization
7. Self-sufficiency
8. Price stability

Social objectives include:

1. Social security
2. Social equality
3. Establishment of socialistic pattern of society

Political objectives are:

1. Establishment of peace
2. Defense

INDUSTRIAL POLICY

The Industrial Policy (IP) plan of a country is its official strategic effort to encourage the development and growth of the manufacturing sector of the economy. The government takes measures aimed at improving the competitiveness and capabilities of domestic firms and promoting structural transformation. A country's infrastructure (transportation, telecommunications and energy industry) is a major part of the manufacturing sector that usually has a key role in IP. It is also the case that industries fail dismally to add to such a growing body of manufacturing industries.

Industrial policies are sector-specific, unlike broader macroeconomic policies. They are often considered to be interventionist as opposed to *laissez-faire* economics. Examples of horizontal, economy-wide policies are tightening credit or taxing capital gain, while examples of vertical, sector-specific policies comprise protecting textiles from imports or subsidizing export industries. Free market advocates consider industrial policies as interventionist measures typical of mixed economy countries.

Role of Department of Industrial Policy and Promotion

The Department of Industrial Policy and Promotion was established in 1995 and has been reconstituted in the year 2000 with the merger of the Department of Industrial Development. Earlier, separate Ministries for Small-scale Industries and Agro and Rural Industries (SSI&A&RI) and Heavy Industries and Public Enterprises (HI&PE) were created in October, 1999.

With progressive liberalization of the Indian economy, initiated in July 1991, there has been a consistent shift in the role and functions of this Department. From regulation and administration of the industrial sector, the role of the Department has been transformed into facilitating investment and technology flows and monitoring industrial development in the liberalized environment.

The role and functions of the Department of Industrial Policy and Promotion primarily include:

- Formulation and implementation of industrial policy and strategies for industrial development in conformity with the development needs and national objectives;
- Monitoring the industrial growth, in general, and performance of industries specifically assigned to it, in particular, including advice on all industrial and technical matters;
- Formulation of Foreign Direct Investment (FDI) Policy and promotion, approval and facilitation of FDI;
- Encouragement to foreign technology collaborations at enterprise level and formulating policy parameters for the same;
- Formulation of policies relating to Intellectual Property Rights in the fields of Patents, Trademarks, Industrial Designs and Geographical Indications of Goods and administration of regulations, rules made thereunder;
- Administration of Industries (Development and Regulation) Act, 1951
- Promoting industrial development of industrially backward areas and the North Eastern Region including International Co-operation for industrial partnerships and
- Promotion of productivity, quality and technical co-operation.

Department of Industrial Policy and Promotion is responsible for formulation and implementation of promotional and developmental measures for growth of the industrial sector, keeping in view the national priorities and socio-economic objectives. While individual Administrative Ministries look after the production, distribution, development and planning aspects of specific industries allocated to them, Department of Industrial Policy and Promotion is responsible for the overall Industrial Policy.

Department of Industrial Policy and Promotion monitors the industrial growth and production, in general, and selected industrial sectors, such as cement, paper and pulp, leather, tyre and rubber, light electrical industries, consumer goods, consumer durables, light machine tools, light industrial machinery, light engineering industries, etc. in particular. Appropriate interventions are made on the basis of policy inputs generated by monitoring and periodic review of the industrial sector. The Department studies, assesses and forecasts the need for technological development in specific industrial sectors. On this basis, it plans for modernization and technological upgradation of the Indian industry so that, it keeps pace with the international developments in industrial technology on a continuing basis.

ROLE OF FEDERATION OF INDIAN CHAMBERS OF COMMERCE AND INDUSTRY (FICCI)

Business views and demands relating to matters of economic planning, as in other matters of economic policy, are communicated to the government through a variety of mechanisms. At the highest level, the Prime Minister is regularly invited and normally attends the annual sessions of the FICCI usually held during the end of March.

FICCI leaders also meet formally and informally with government ministers and other officials. Additionally, the organization has a special officer to keep close contact with members of Parliament. FICCI members also represent the organization's viewpoint in government advisory bodies, such as the Central Advisory Council on industries. The organization sends memoranda, representations, brochures and pamphlets to the government and its constituted ministries.

The Federation of Indian Chambers of Commerce and Industry (FICCI) is an association of business organizations in India. Established in 1927, by G.D. Birla and Purushottam Das Thakurdas, it is the largest, oldest and the apex business organization in India. It is a non-government, not-for-profit organization. FICCI draws its membership from the corporate sector, both private and public, including SMEs and MNCs. The chamber has an indirect membership of over 2,50,000 companies from various regional chambers of commerce. It is involved in sector-specific business policy consensus building, and business promotion and networking. It is headquartered in New Delhi and has presence in 11 states in India and 8 countries across the world.

CONFEDERATION OF INDIAN INDUSTRIES (CII)

The Confederation of Indian Industries (CII) works to create and sustain an environment conducive to the development of India, partnering industry, Government, and civil society, through advisory and consultative processes.

CII is a non-government, not-for-profit, industry-led and industry-managed organization, playing a proactive role in India's development process. Founded in 1895, India's premier business association has over 7200 members, from the private as well as public sectors, including SMEs and MNCs, and an indirect membership of over 100,000 enterprises from around 242 national and regional sectoral industry bodies.

With 64 offices, including 9 Centres of Excellence, in India, and 7 overseas offices in Australia, China, Egypt, France, Singapore, UK, and USA as well as institutional partnerships with 312 counterpart organizations in 106 countries, CII serves as a reference point for Indian industry and the international business community.

CII Functions

Functions of CII include:

1. Charting change by working closely with Government on policy issues, interfacing with thought leaders, and enhancing efficiency, competitiveness and business opportunities for industry through a range of specialized services and strategic global linkages. It also provides a

platform for consensus-building and networking on key issues.

2. Extending its agenda beyond business, CII assists industry to identify and execute corporate citizenship programs. Partnerships with civil society organizations carry forward corporate initiatives for integrated and inclusive development across diverse domains including affirmative action, healthcare, education, livelihood, diversity management, skill development, empowerment of women, to name a few.

3. The CII theme of 'Accelerating Growth, Creating Employment' for 2014-15 aims to strengthen a growth process that meets the aspirations of today's India. During the year, CII will specially focus on economic growth, education, skill development, manufacturing, investments, ease of doing business, export competitiveness, legal and regulatory architecture, labour law reforms and entrepreneurship as growth enablers.

4. The CII Research team regularly tracks economic, political and business developments within India and abroad to comment on the emerging economic scenario for the Indian corporate sector. With the mandate to keep members updated on economic, political and business conditions across the country and abroad, the CII Research team:
   - Tracks emerging developments in the domestic and international economic space.
   - Comments on policy developments to analyze the immediate as well as long-term impact of policy changes.
   - Presents comprehensive industry analysis to understand the industry dynamics and assess the growth potential and profitability in the broad regulatory and policy environment.
   - Conducts surveys to reflect business conditions and sentiment.

5. CII Research is also well versed and well equipped to offer customized research-based consultancy services on any

theme. It has been catering to the needs of various stakeholders including industries, business houses and government providing meaningful insights about the prevailing trends, outlook on likely future trends, factors behind these trends, existing government policies and policy recommendations with an objective to help stakeholders in better understanding of the issues at hand. The objective of CII Research is to assist stakeholders in taking more informed and strategic decisions with due focus on the attainment of short-term as well as long-term goals.

6. International outreach: CII international undertakes activities to connect Indian business with global business. Such activities include meeting the Heads of State and Government, decision-makers, networking with counterpart organizations, multilateral and academic institutions and other policy making bodies

7. CII's International Department is committed to stepping up its engagement with the world on a wide range of issues that it identifies as being national priorities of corporate India.

CHECK YOUR UNDERSTANDING

1. What do you mean by business and its environment? Explain the concept of internal and external environment.
2. Explain the components of economic environment.
3. What is the philosophy of economic growth of India and its implications on business?
4. Explain the main features of economic planning.
5. What is the purpose of economic planning for a developing country?
6. What is the role of industrial policy? How the government regulates the business through the policy?
7. Write short note on the role of FICCI and CII.

REFERENCES

1. Goyal Alok *et al.*: Business Environment, VK (India) Enterprises, New Delhi.
2. Ashwathappa, K.: Essentials of Business Environment, Himalaya Publishing House, Mumbai.
3. Acharya B.K. and Govekar, P.B.: Business Policy and Strategic Management, Himalaya Publishing House, Mumbai.
4. http://www.ficci.com
5. http://www.cii.in

Chapter

7

Corporate Social Responsibility

This Chapter deals with:

- Definition
- Evolution
- Need for CSR
- Theoretical Perspectives
- Corporate Citizenships
- Business Practices
- Strategies for CSR
- Challenges and Implementation

INTRODUCTION

Modern business is large and complex catering to national and even global markets. It exercises a definite and extensive influence on our economic and social lifestyles. As a socio-economic institution a company has to perform all tasks involved in the development and delivery of desirable goods and services from production to consumption. As a social institution, it is responsible to deliver a standard of living and maximize life quality. Now, life quality means not only quality and quantity of consumer goods and services but also enriched quality of the life in society and the environment.

DEFINITIONS

What is Corporate Social Responsibility (CSR)? It is not as simple as it sounds. The definitions differ vastly according to the perception and sensitivity of the analyst. Some of the definitions are given below:

The World Business Council for Sustainable Development – CSR is the continuing commitment by business to behave ethically and contribute to economic development while improving quality of life of the workforce and their families as well as of the local community and society at large.

The same report gave some evidence of the different perceptions of what this should mean from a number of different societies across the world. In the United States, CSR has been defined traditionally much more in terms of philanthropic mode. Companies make profits unhindered except by fulfilling their duty to pay taxes. Then they donate a certain share of the profits to charitable causes. It is seen as tainting the act for the company to receive any benefit from the giving. The European model is much more focused on operating the core business in a socially responsible way, complemented by investment in communities for social business case reasons. It is believed that this model is more sustainable because: (i) Social responsibility becomes an integral part of the wealth creation process, which if managed properly should enhance the competitiveness of business and maximize the value of wealth creation to society; (ii) When time gets hard, there is the incentive to practice CSR more and better, if it is a philanthropic exercise which is peripheral to the main business, it will always be the first thing to go.

But as with any process based on the collective activities of communities of human beings (as companies are), there is no "one size fits all". In different countries, there will be different priorities and values that will shape how business acts. (i) Today, leading practitioners of CSR believe that CSR is an integral part of the wealth creation process and should enhance competitiveness of business and help the company in times of crisis; (ii) the stakeholder theory of CSR stresses that it is a manager's duty to balance the shareholders' financial interests against the interest of other stakeholders, such as employees, customers and the local community.

Nobel laureate, economist Milton Friedman, says: "There is one and only one social responsibility of business – to use its resources and engage in activities designed to increase its profits so long as it engages in open and free competition, without deception or fraud." To Henry Ford, " The purpose of business is to do as much good as we can, everywhere for everybody concerned... and incidentally to make money". No wonder the meaning of the concept of Corporate Social Responsibility seems to differ from person to person according to their own sensitivity.

To Manmohan Singh, Prime Minister of India, "Corporate social responsibility is no philanthropy. It is not charity. It is an investment in our collective future".

The simplest and the most significant definition of CSR was given by Mahatma Gandhi who said: Wealth created from society has to be ploughed back into society. The sum and substance of all these definitions can be put into following propositions:

(i) It is an attempt made by companies to be voluntarily responsible to ethical and social considerations.

It is not legal binding for the company, unlike corporate accountability (which makes company adhere to legal and social norms).

(ii) Obligations to pursue those policies, to make those decisions, or to follow those lines of action which are desirable in terms of the objectives and values of our society.

(iii) The set of obligations an organization has to project, enhance, and otherwise work to the betterment of the society in which it functions.

(iv) CSR is the overall relationship of the corporate with all of its stakeholders. These include customers, employees, communities, owners/investors, government, suppliers and competitors. Elements of social responsibility include investment in community outreach, employee relations, creation and maintenance of employment, environmental stewardship and financial performance.

(v) The social responsibility of business encompasses the economic, legal, ethical and discretionary expectations placed on organizations by society at a given point of time.

Today, we also insist on the social responsiveness of management which means the ability and willingness of management to relate the plans and policies to the social environment in such ways that are mutually beneficial to the organization and to society. The social responsiveness implies actions and the 'how' of the responses of the management. The current trend is in company's involvement in social actions. The mission of a corporation expresses such involvement in social actions to improve the quality of life. Any enterprise must interact with, and live in, as a responsible citizen in the society. In an age of fast changing and turbulent environment, pro-action on the part of management is demanded to meet the challenges faced by the society.

EVOLUTION

The Industrial Revolution was a period of change and transformation from hand-made items to machine-made and mass-produced goods. The change brought both positive and negative effects in general life. There was a rise in pollution levels, working conditions declined, and there was an increase in the number of working women and children. Two revolutions that took place resulted in both productive and dire consequences. The meaning of CSR has been changing from the days to the Industrial Revolution. As the world business environment is changing, the requirements for success and competitiveness are also changing. As a result, large corporations are emphasizing the maintenance of strategic relationships with different sections of the society. In the process, the corporate social responsibility is gaining importance.

Evolution of CRS in India

India has the world's richest tradition of Corporate Social Responsibility (CSR). The term CSR may be relatively new to India, but the concept dates back to Mauryan history, where philosophers like Kautilya emphasized on ethical practices and principles while conducting business. CSR has been informally practiced in ancient times in the form of charity to the poor and disadvantaged. Indian scriptures have at several places mentioned the importance of sharing one's earning with the deprived section of society. We have a deep rooted culture of sharing and caring.

Religion also played a major role in promoting the concept of CSR. Islam had a law called Zakaat, which rules that a portion of one's earning must be shared with the poor in form of donations. Merchants belonging to Hindu religion gave alms, got temples and night shelters made for the poorer class. Hindus followed Dharmada where the manufacturer or seller charged a specific amount from the purchaser, which was used for charity. The amount was known as charity amount or Dharmada. In the same fashion, Sikhs followed Daashaant.

Here, we can understand that the history of CSR in India runs parallel to the historical development of India. CSR has evolved in phases like community engagement, socially responsible production, and socially responsible employee relations. Therefore, the history of Corporate Social Responsibility in India can be broadly divided into four phases:

The first phase of CSR was driven by noble deeds of philanthropists and charity. It was influenced by family values, traditions, culture and religion along with industrialization. Till 1850, the wealthy businessmen shared their riches with the society by either setting up temples or religious institutions. In times of famines, they opened their granaries for the poor and hungry. The approach towards CSR changed with the arrival of colonial rule in 1850. In the Pre-independence era, the pioneers or propagators of industrialization also supported the concept of CSR. In 1900s, the industrialist families like Tatas, Birlas, Modis, Godrej, Bajajs and Singhanias promoted this concept by setting up charitable foundations, educational and healthcare institutions, and trusts for community development. It may also be interesting to note that their efforts for social benefit were also driven by political motives.

The second phase was the period of independence struggle when the industrialists were pressurized to show their dedication towards the benefit of the society. Mahatma Gandhi urged to the powerful industrialists to share their wealth for the benefit of underprivileged section of the society. He gave the concept of trusteeship. This concept of trusteeship helped in the socio-economic growth of India. Gandhi regarded the Indian companies and industries as "Temples of Modern India". He influenced the industrialists and business houses to build trusts for colleges, research and training institutes. These trusts also worked to enhance social reforms like rural development, women empowerment and education.

In the third phase from 1960-80, CSR was influenced by the emergence of public sector undertakings to ensure proper distribution of wealth. The policy of industrial licensing, high taxes and restrictions on the private sector resulted in corporate malpractices. This led to enactment of legislation regarding corporate governance, labour and environmental issues. Still the PSUs were not very successful. Therefore, there was a natural shift of expectation from the public to the private sector and their active involvement in the socio-economic growth. In 1965, the academicians, politicians and businessmen set up a national workshop on CSR, where great stress was laid on social accountability and transparency.

In the fourth phase from 1980 onwards, Indian companies integrated CSR into a sustainable business strategy. With globalization and economic liberalization in 1990s, and partial withdrawal of controls and licensing systems, there was a boom in the economic growth of the country. This led to the increased momentum in industrial growth, making it possible for the companies to contribute more towards social responsibility. What started as charity is now understood and accepted as responsibility.

In the current scenario in India, the new Companies Act amended in December 2012 mandates the corporate to spend 2 per cent of their average net profits of the last three financial years towards CSR. This is applicable for companies with a turnover of 1000 crores/PAT of 5 crores/or net worth of 500 crores. The new bill replaces the Companies Act 1956 and emphasizes carrying forward the agenda of Corporate Social Responsibility.

On the other hand, it is mandatory for Central Public Sector Enterprises to allocate 2-3 per cent of the PAT for the inclusive development of a backward district (CSR and Sustainability Guidelines by Department of Public Enterprises 2013). Thus, the country is at the verge of beginning a interesting stakeholder relationship through Corporate Social Responsibility programmes which would arise into inclusive and equitable growth and benefit the needy and the underprivileged across the country.

As discussed above, CSR is not a new concept in India. Ever since their inception, corporates like the Tata Group, the Aditya Birla Group, and Indian Oil Corporation, to name a few, have been involved in serving the community. Through donations and charity events, many other organizations have been doing their part for the society. The basic objective of CSR in these days is to maximize the company's overall impact on the society and stakeholders. CSR policies, practices and programmes are being comprehensively integrated by an increasing number of companies throughout their business operations and processes. A growing number of corporates feel that CSR is not just another form of indirect expense but is important for protecting the goodwill and reputation, defending attacks and increasing business competitiveness.

Companies have specialized CSR teams that formulate policies, strategies and goals for their CSR programmes and set aside budgets to fund them. These programmes are often determined by social philosophy which have clear objectives and are well-defined and are aligned with the mainstream business. The programmes are put into practice by the employees who are crucial to this process. CSR programmes ranges from community development to development in education, environment and healthcare etc.

For example, a more comprehensive method of development is adopted by some corporations such as Bharat Petroleum Corporation Limited and Maruti Suzuki India Limited. Provision of improved medical and sanitation facilities, building schools and houses, and empowering the villagers and in process making them more self-reliant by providing vocational training and a knowledge of business operations are the facilities that these corporations focus on. Many of the companies are helping other peoples by providing them good standard of living.

Also, corporates increasingly join hands with non-governmental organizations (NGOs) and use their expertise in devising programmes which address wider social problems.

CSR has gone through many phases in India. The ability to make a significant difference in the society and improve the overall quality of life has clearly been proven by the corporates. Not one but all corporates should try and bring about a change in the current social situation in India in order to have an effective and lasting solution to the social woes. Partnerships between companies, NGOs and the government should be facilitated so that a combination of their skills such as expertise, strategic thinking, manpower and money to initiate extensive social change will put the socio-economic development of India on a fast track.

NEED FOR CSR

Corporates work towards the single-minded pursuit of profit. Profit maximization by the continued increase of efficiency is the most socially responsible way of conducting business. This implies making quick money, with utter disregard for the responsibility of business towards society. This limited view of business would be counterproductive in the long run. But on the other hand, the long-range view of business, which would imply an aim at the long-term gains rather than at quick returns, would take into account the important dimension of social responsibility.

James Burke, the chairman of the well-known consumer product and pharmaceutical company, Johnson & Johnson said this: “I have long harboured the belief that the most successful corporations in this country, the ones that have delivered outstanding results over a long period of time, were driven by a simple moral imperative, namely serving the public in the broadest possible sense better than their competitors”.

If we are to compete effectively in the global marketplace, corporations must take along, hard look at their values, practices and assumptions. They need to question their accepted modes of behaviour, promulgating new values and set up new standards of conduct which are openly held and shared within the corporation, while proclaimed to the outside world.

Accountability to Society: There is yet another reason why corporations should be conscious of their “social responsibility”. In a democratic society, any kind of enterprise exists for the sake of society. If private enterprise is justified and allowed to exist, it is because it is seen to contribute better than public enterprise to the common good. It produces better goods and functions more efficiently, thanks to the encouragement given to individual initiatives. At the same time, private enterprise is not encouraged because individuals may accumulate wealth for their own exclusive and selfish benefit at the expense of the public.

Industries are allowed to exist because they are perceived by the public to be useful in the attainment of the personal, social and material goals of the people. It is because of this ethical perception that the employees of TISCO and the general public protested in 1977 when the then Union Minister for Industry, George Fernandes attempted to nationalize TISCO. On the other hand, when the public perceives that certain corporations do not function in the general interest of the nation, it does not object to their take over by the government, as it happened in the nationalization of the coal fields, the oil industry and Indian Copper Corporation. Since corporations exist for the sake of the public, they are accountable to the public and have a social responsibility.

Debt to Society: Corporation whether public or private draw much from society. No corporation is an island in itself. It depends on society for the developed infrastructure such as roads, water supply, electricity and an educated workforce. It also depends on society for the maintenance of law and order, public health, transport facilities and for its reaching out to its customers through mass media. Finally, all consumers of its finished products are drawn from society.

If a corporation draws so much from society, it has to make its contribution to society. It has a debt to pay to the society. In the first place, a corporation has to behave like a good citizen. This is to be shown in the faithful and full payment of taxes, the observation of all local and national laws and perhaps even going beyond the law in matters of pollution, quality of product, safety and energy and resource conservation. The corporation has to donate generously towards causes of public welfare and must get itself directly involved in social welfare programmes.

It is because of these aspects of social responsibility and public accountability that corporations have to take into account not only the interests of its shareholders, but also those of the workers, consumers, suppliers, the government and the general public who are its stakeholders. In short, corporations because of their social responsibility have to consider themselves the "custodian of public welfare" .

Consumers increasingly don't accept unethical business practices or organizations who act irresponsibly. Advances in social media (giving everyone a voice) mean that negative or destructive practices quickly fuel conversations online. Organizations are accountable for their actions like never before.

The Business Benefits of CSR

CSR should not be viewed as a drain on resources, because carefully implemented CSR policies can help the organization:

- Win new business
- Increase customer retention

- Develop and enhance relationships with customers, suppliers and networks
- Attract, retain and maintain a happy workforce and be an Employer of Choice
- Save money on energy and operating costs and manage risk
- Differentiate yourself from your competitors
- Generate innovation and learning and enhance your influence
- Improve your business reputation and standing
- Provide access to investment and funding opportunities
- Generate positive publicity and media opportunities due to media interest in ethical business activities

THEORETICAL PERSPECTIVES

Social scientists have formulated several theories that justify the importance of corporates engaged in promoting social welfare of the society in which they operate. The following sections describe these theories:

The Trusteeship Model

The Trusteeship Model adopts a realistic and descriptive perspective in viewing the current governing situation of a publicly held corporation, drawing from the continental European conception of the corporation as a social institution with a corporate personality.

Kay and Silberston (1995) argue that a public corporation is not the creation of a private contract and thus not owned by any individual. Ownership is by definition where the owner has exclusive rights of possession, use, gain and legal disposition of a material object. Yet shareholders merely own their shares in a company and trade their shares with others in the stock market. They do not have rights to possess and use the assets of the company, to make decision about the direction of the company, and to transfer the assets of the company to others. The residual claims of the shareholders are determined by the company and if the company's performance does not satisfy the shareholders requirements, the shareholders are left with a single option of "exit" rather than "voice" as shareholders, in general are in no way able to monitor the management effectively and neither are interested in running the corporate business. In this sense, the assumption that the corporation is owned by the shareholders is in fact meaningless. For Kay and Silberston, ownership rights are not important to business. Many public institutions such as museums, universities, and libraries perform will without clear owners.

Indeed, the Indian Company Law does not explicitly grant shareholders ownership rights because the corporation is regarded as an independent legal person separate from its members, and shareholders are merely the "residual claimants" of the corporation. The company has its own assets, rights and duties, and has its own will and capacity to act and is responsible for its own actions. Therefore, Kay and Silberston reject the idea that managements are the agents of shareholders. The trusteeship model differs from the agency model in two ways: Firstly, the fiduciary duty of the trustees is to sustain the corporation's assets including not only the shareholders' wealth, but also broader stakeholders' value such as the skills of employees, the expectations of customers and suppliers, and the company's reputation in the community. Managers as trustees are to promote the boarder interest of the corporation as a whole, not solely the financial interest of its shareholders. Second, managers have to balance the conflicting interest of current and future stakeholder and to develop the company's capacities in a long-term perspective rather than focus on short-term shareholder gains. To establish a trusteeship model, they ask for statutory changes in corporate governance, such as changing the current statutory duties of the directors, ensuring the power of independent directors to nominate directors and select senior managers and appoint CEOs for a fixed 4 year term and so on.

The Social Entity Theory

The theory has, in recent years, been promoted by three major social thinkers – the Democratic Political theorist, Robert Dahl (1985) using economic democracy, Paul Hirst (1994) using associationalism, and Jonathan Boswell (1990) using communication notion of property. The social entity conception of the corporation regards the company not as a private association united by individual property rights, but as a public association constituted through political and legal processes and as a social entity for pursuing collective goals with public objections. The social entity theory views the corporation as a social institution in society based on the grounds of fundamental value and moral order of the community. " With the fundamental value of human rights, and standard of a corporation's usefulness is not whether it creates individual wealth, but sense of the meaning of the community by honouring individual dignity and promoting over all welfare". Sullivan argues that corporation are granted charter entity for a commercial purpose, but more importantly, as a social entity, for general community needs. The corporation identity and executives are representatives and guardians of all corporate stakeholder's interests.

The recent resurgence of the moral aspect of stakeholder perspectives has been, in general, associated with the social entity conception of the corporation.

The Pluralistic Model

The Pluralistic Model supports the idea of multiple interests of stakeholders, rather than shareholder interest alone. It argues that the corporation should serve and accommodate wider stakeholder interest in order to make the corporation more efficient and legitimate.

It suggests that corporate governance should not move away from ownership rights, but that such rights should not be solely claimed by, and thus concentrated in, shareholders' ownership right can also be claimed by other stakeholders, particularly employees. Stakeholders who make firm specific investments and contributions and bear risks in the corporation should have residual claims and should participate in the corporate decision-making to enhance corporate efficiency.

It is asserted that if corporations practice stakeholder management, their growth and profitability will increase and they will be more stable.

CORPORATE CITIZENSHIP

Corporate Citizenship is the extent to which businesses are socially responsible for meeting legal, ethical and economic responsibilities placed on them by shareholders. As demand for socially responsible corporations increases, investors, consumers and employees are now more willing to use their individual power to punish companies that do not share their values. For example, investors who find out about a company's negative corporate citizenship practices could boycott its products or services, refuse to invest in its stock or speak out against that company among family and friends.

Corporate Citizenship is a recognition that a business, corporation or business-like organization, has social, cultural and environmental responsibilities to the community in which it seeks a licence to operate as well as economic and financial ones to its shareholders or immediate stakeholders. Corporate citizenship involves an organization coming to terms with the need for, often, radical internal and external changes, in order to better meet its responsibilities to all of its stakeholders (direct or indirect), in order to establish, and maintain, sustainable success for the organization, and, as a result of that success, to achieve long-term sustainable success for the community at large.

A corporation is a creation of law as an association of persons forming part of the society in which it operates. Its activities are bound to impact the society as the society's value would have an impact on the corporation. Therefore, they have mutual rights and obligations to discharge for the benefit of each other.

A corporation should be committed to be a good corporate citizen not only in compliance with all relevant laws and regulations, but also by actively assisting in the improvement of the quality of life of the people in the communities in which it operates with the objective of making them self-reliant and enjoy a better quality of life. Such social commitment consists of initiating and supporting community initiatives in the field of public health and family welfare, water management, vocational training, education and literacy and encourages application of modern scientific and managerial techniques and expertise. The company should review its policy in this respect periodically in consonance with national and regional priorities. The company should strive to incorporate them as an integral part of its business plan and not treat them as optional and some thing dispensed with when inconvenient. It should encourage volunteering amongst its employees and help them to work in the communities. The company should develop social accounting systems and carry out social audit of its operations towards the community, employees and shareholders.

Corporate citizenship, also referred to as corporate social responsibility, is increasingly instrumental in defining the role of business in society. As the issue of integrating broader economic, environmental, and social concerns into evaluating corporate performance gains prominence, proper understanding of what it means for a company to be a good citizen becomes crucial.

Corporate citizenship is a contribution a company makes to society and the environment in which it conducts business. Traditionally, it has been understood as philanthropy and investment in social causes. But corporate citizenship has a broader meaning, including the benefits of a company's core business activities to local communities, as well as civic engagement that helps the economy and the society as a whole. Corporate citizenship is not only about obligations, it's also about rights. It is about how the private sector can prosper and at the same time improve the environment it operates in. Globally competitive business cannot exist in failed, unstable, corrupt, undemocratic countries.

For corporate citizenship to be effective, it has to move beyond being showcased as a public affairs strategy and instead it must become an integral part of business strategy. It means looking beyond short-term profits and working to reduce poverty, fight serious diseases such as HIV/AIDS or malaria, support education, protect the environment, advance ethical standards, and promote good business environment. Therefore, corporate citizenship should go beyond immediate financial contributions to charitable causes and prompt companies to become active members of the society working together with other stakeholders on crucial policy issues.

BUSINESS PRACTICES

A method, procedure, process, or rule employed or followed by a company in the pursuit of its objectives. Business practice may also refer to these collectively. A set of guidelines, ethics or ideas that represent the most efficient or prudent course of action. Best practices are often set forth by an authority, such as a governing body or management, depending on the circumstances. While best practices generally dictate the recommended course of action, some situations require that such practices be followed.

Colgate – Business Practices Guidelines

Our Business Practices Guidelines illustrate how the values and principles outlined in the Colgate Code of Conduct apply to particular business situations. Our guidelines detail not only Colgate policies but also our company's compliance with specific laws, regulations and practices.

Topics addressed by our Business Practices Guidelines include:

- International business activities
- Conflicts of interest
- Antitrust and trade regulations
- Environmental, health and safety principles
- Product safety research
- Advertising guidelines and placement policies
- Proprietary company information

Ethical business practices are actions performed and attitudes held by a business and its employees that are considered professionally and morally responsible. These types of practices typically seek to promote the goals of the company without sacrificing the common good of its employees, customers, and even competitors. This often includes programmes to ensure fair hiring and promotion within a company, treating customers fairly, and being honest in regard to programmes to increase sales. Ethical practices are often initiated as a "top down" programme, with corporate officers and the heads of the company acting as role models of behaviour for other employees.

For many companies, ethical business practices do not have to disrupt the pursuit of profits and professional growth. There is often an incorrect assumption that a business should do anything to make money and get ahead, but many companies have been successful while still acting in a way that is ethical and serves the common good as well as the corporate good. These sorts of business practices can begin with programmes that donate money to charities or other needy organizations, and extend to how customers and employees are treated by a company.

Many ethical business practices are related to how employees within a company are hired, treated, and promoted. This often includes policies that discourage discrimination, attempt to avoid issues regarding fraternization between different levels of employees, and seek to find fair ways to settle conflict within the company. These practices also often include ensuring employees are given reasonable working conditions, are treated with respect, and have any investments toward retirement protected appropriately. These practices often include treating customers with respect and honesty, not using personal information provided by customers in unscrupulous ways, and charging customers fairly for goods or services. When these types of practices are not observed or are broken, many customers show their dissatisfaction by no longer giving the company their business.

One of the best ways to implement and ensure the proper establishment of ethical business practices is as a "top down" programme. Those at the top of a company are often seen as professional role models for other employees, and if they are acting in a way that is unethical, many lower level employees will follow suit. This can lead to additional costs to a company due to theft, reduced productivity, and potential lawsuits. There may also be negative consequences for the value of a publicly traded company if the officers in charge of the company are unethical.

STRATEGIES FOR CSR

Serious companies know that they need strategies to achieve their mainline business goals; many companies also know that they need to develop strategies for their CSR goals as well. However, because the goals for most CSR efforts aren't in support of typical corporate functions such as marketing, manufacturing, sales, and so forth, many companies are unsure of what goals to set for CSR efforts or what strategies to pursue. The result is often a hodgepodge of unfocused, unconnected, and unrelated strategies in search of an overarching goal.

Developing an Effective CSR Strategy

At a minimum, companies should focus on the following set of good practices as they craft their own CSR goals.

Senior leadership and management of the firm, including the board of directors, must make an authentic, firm, and public commitment to CSR efforts, and engage with them. Often, CSR efforts will be born organically throughout lower levels of employees. But even if they are, at some stage senior executives have to be brought on board, have to commit to them, and have to engage with them. This clear vision of CSR needs to be embedded within the core values of the firm and reflect those values, and it must be linked to the mission, vision, and values of the organization. And this core vision needs to openly recognize that CSR is central to creating not only social or environmental value but also to creating business value. Firms must be unabashedly unapologetic about that. CSR efforts should be treated and managed as core business strategy, just as are the strategies of marketing, research and development, capital expenditure, and talent management.

Determine the top three business objectives of the company and develop CSR goals that will contribute to the achievement of those business objectives. In developing CSR goals, the company must determine what its business objectives are. Defining business objectives is not as easy an exercise as it might appear to be at first glance. Often when five business managers from the same firm are asked to describe their business objectives and priorities, they give five different answers. For example, I worked with a tech company in Silicon Valley whose top executive quickly answered the top three business objectives question: "Growth, growth, and growth." Her human resources director looked quite pained in responding that until they were able to rein in the company's high turnover rate, they were going to have a difficult time growing, growing, growing.

A CEO might say that the most pressing objective is to increase market share or increase sales, while the human resources leader might say that it is to recruit and attract the best talent, engage and unify disparate employee silos and business units, or improve employee satisfaction. The conversation needs to happen at a deeper level so that the CSR goals can serve these general objectives. Is the objective to grow in new markets? If so, which ones? Is it to penetrate new customer segments or grab market share from competitors? If so, which market segments? After business objectives are determined, align CSR goals with the firm's core competencies. This practice requires focus and discipline. Typically, CSR is executed in an ad hoc, non-integrated fashion. CSR initiatives can originate in all parts of an organization and if mapped are often not linked to what the firm actually knows, does, or is expert in. CSR can come from the passion of a CEO or a motivated employee. It can come simply from the causes and issues whose representative organizations (often non-profits) ask the firm for support. Firms should, however, seek causes and social or environmental strategies for which they own part of the solution.

The classic case is Ford Motor Company Fund's support for breast cancer research—to the tune of $ 95 million over fourteen years to Susan G. Komen for the cure. There is no argument that this is an eminently worthy cause that meets a significant need, and it is only one of many programmes that Ford supports in its CSR effort. But it is an important part of Ford's CSR effort, and there is no strategic link between the company's support for breast cancer research and the building of cars and trucks. Automotive companies know cars, transportation engineering, and design, so perhaps support for alternatively fueled vehicles and addressing the global and environmental challenges around gasoline dependency are more fitting to the firm's core competencies and business objectives of selling more cars. Not only may Ford be in a better market position if it focuses on more strategically aligned causes, but the results of its initiatives in these areas may lead to the development of innovative new automotive technologies, which will lead to new products and revenue streams.

Fully integrate CSR efforts into the governance of the company and into existing management systems. If CSR efforts are not built into the performance appraisal system for a company's employees, for example, then the chances are good that they will not be fully embraced and executed with the precision of the commonly measured functions such as sales and staff management. You should view CSR as both a risk-mitigation strategy and an opportunity-seeking strategy. Seek to find the sweet spot, that is, the intersection between business and social or environmental returns. Seek out partners in the community who have developed deep expertise in the cause or issue you are targeting, and work with these organizations, usually in the non-profit sector, to develop the best solution and build capacity.

Non-profit partners are also in a better position to help the company communicate its CSR efforts, as non-profits enjoy a higher level of trust. Finally, develop clear performance metrics, or key performance indicators, to measure the impact of your CSR efforts. These metrics should be both internal (measuring reputation, market share, brand perception, sales, operating expenses, and employee satisfaction) and external (measuring achievements in society and the environment). If no performance metrics are in place, you will have no way to prove that the effort was effective, and it will not be sustainable over the long haul.

CHALLENGES AND IMPLEMENTATION

There are four models of corporate responsibility globally. In the first model, whose major proponent was Mahatma Gandhi, the emphasis is on companies taking to public welfare on their own volition, without any prodding from external agencies such as the government. In the second model, Pandit Jawaharlal Nehru, the votary of state ownership of enterprises, held the view that public ownership and legal requirements that govern them define CSR, In the liberal model of CSR, whose proponent was Milton Friedman held the view that CSR is limited to private owners and not to other stakeholders. Finally, the stakeholder model, as propounded by Edward Freeman, emphasizes the view that companies should respond to the needs of all stakeholders.

The aim of CSR is to aid the continuity of the business in terms of results, reputation, network participation and the reduction of risks. This has to be translated into strategies, primary processes, employee behaviour and the development of suitable competences. Until now, businesses have primarily drawn on the paradigm developed in the industrial age. The present political, social and organizational situation indicates that a re-examination of this paradigm is necessary.

In the current global conversation, CSR tends to be as much about semantics as substance. The fundamental idea that drives for change should be found primarily within the heart of organizations and expressed through various implementation strategies. As long as organizations are not embracing CSR as a fundamental element in business continuity, it will remain a mixture of semantics, avoidance, compliance and social philanthropy.

Challenges include:

(i) Corporates have to develop a better understanding of the strategic, tactical and operational translation of CSR into the core of the organization. Any thing done without involvement will remain a dry execution with no results.

(ii) The core issue is how to organize systematic and transparent interactions with a growing number of stakeholders and the issues they represent, but how these concerns can be embedded appropriately in the organization remains unclear. Understanding what it implies to (re)organize in order systematically to take into account this wider context and its constituencies.

(iii) Semantics and window-dressing are often combined with a modern variation of social philanthropy. The central mantra is 'We are doing good" by "Introduction doing well'. Examples are the purchase of Christmas gift packages from less developed countries and products from Max Havelaar. Research shows that a majority of businesses have recently learned to adapt their business language to the vocabulary of CSR, and social philanthropy has always existed. Although there is nothing wrong with all this, it does not really go to the heart of CSR.

(iv) CSR is treated as an act of compliance, of conforming to rules and regulations and doing what the law requires one to do. However, the growing number of corporate scandals makes it clear that complying with the law is not always taken seriously.

(v) A CSR strategy that is focused on avoiding regulatory liability and maintaining a license to operate in the current business will neither lead to current competitive advantage nor an imagination of future business models.

(vi) Many companies think that corporate social responsibility is a peripheral issue for their business and customer satisfaction more important for them. They imagine that customer satisfaction is now only about price and service, but they fail to recognize on important changes that are taking place worldwide that could blow the business out of the water.

(vii) Lack of community participation in CSR activities: There is a lack of interest of the local community in participating and contributing to CSR activities of companies. This is largely attributable to the fact that there exists little or no knowledge about CSR within the local communities as no serious efforts have been made to spread awareness about CSR and instill confidence in the local communities about such initiatives. The situation is further aggravated by a lack of communication between the company and the community at the grassroots.

(viii) Need to build local capacities: There is a need for capacity building of the local non-governmental organizations as there is serious dearth of trained and efficient organizations that can effectively contribute to the ongoing CSR activities initiated by companies. This seriously compromises scaling up of CSR initiatives and subsequently limits the scope of such activities.

(ix) Issues of transparency: Lack of transparency is one of the key issues brought forth by one survey. There is an expression by the companies that there exists lack of transparency on the part of the local implementing agencies as they do not make adequate efforts to disclose information on their programmes.

(x) Audit issues, impact assessment and utilization of funds. This reported lack of transparency negatively impacts the process of trust building between companies and local communities, which is a key to the success of any CSR initiative at the local level.

(xi) Non-availability of well organized non-governmental organizations: It is also reported that there is non-availability of well organized non-governmental organizations in remote and rural areas that can assess and identify real needs of the community and work along with companies to ensure successful implementation of CSR activities. This also builds the case for investing in local communities by way of building their capacities to undertake development projects at local levels.

(xii) Visibility factor: The role of media in highlighting good cases of successful CSR initiatives is welcomed as it spreads good stories and sensitizes the local population about various ongoing CSR initiatives of companies. This apparent influence of gaining visibility and branding exercise often leads many nongovernmental organizations to involve themselves in event-based programmes; in the process, they often miss out on meaningful grassroots interventions.

(xiii) Narrow perception towards CSR initiatives: Non-governmental organizations and Government agencies usually possess a narrow outlook towards the CSR initiatives of companies, often defining CSR initiatives more donor-driven than local in approach. As a result, they find it hard to decide whether they should participate in such activities at all in medium and long run.

(xiv) Non-availability of clear CSR Guidelines: There are no clear-cut statutory guidelines or policy directives to give a definitive direction to CSR initiatives of companies. It is found that the scale of CSR initiatives of companies should depend upon their business size and profile. In other words, the bigger the company, the bigger is its CSR programme.

(xv) Lack of consensus on implementing CSR issues: There is a lack of consensus amongst local agencies regarding CSR projects. This lack of consensus often results in duplication of activities by corporate houses in areas of their intervention. This results in a competitive spirit between local implementing agencies rather than building collaborative approaches on issues. This factor limits company's abilities to undertake impact assessment of their initiatives from time to time.

IMPLEMENTATION

CSR initiatives are executed by corporate in partnership with Non-governmental Organizations (NGOs) who are well versed in working with the local communities and are experts in tackling specific social problems. Companies can associate the NGO in selecting the projects since NGOs are well versed with the local communities of the identified geography. As companies go forward in CSR, they can develop their own expertise in project implementation so that there is continuous involvement from the companies side. When the CSR team is selected, if right people with passion are selected, there will be better result. Hence, implementation process can improve.

CHECK YOUR UNDERSTANDING

1. Define corporate social responsibility and explain the rationale.
2. What is the need for CSR and what are the pros and cons of the initiative?
3. What is corporate citizenship and what is the reasoning for such concept?
4. What are the challenges for CSR? Explain the strategies for implementation.

REFERENCES

1. Riya Rupani: Business Ethics and Corporate Governance, Himalaya Publishing House Pvt. Ltd., Mumbai.
2. Bhat Govinda K. Dr. and Sumitha Ayodhya: Business Ethics and Corporate Social Responsibility, Himalaya Publishing House Pvt. Ltd., Mumbai.
3. The Institute of Chartered Financial Analysts of India: Business Ethics and Corporate Governance, ICFAI Centre for Management Research, Hyderabad - 500034.
4. Gupta, C.B.: Business Ethics and Communication, Sultan Chand & Sons, New Delhi, http://www.cauxroundtable.org

This Chapter deals with:

- Evolution of Corporate Governance
- Governance Practices and Regulations
- Structure and Development of Boards
- Role of Capital Market and Government
- Governance Rating
- Future of Governance – Innovative Practices
- Case Studies with Lessons Learnt

INTRODUCTION

Corporate Governance is essentially all about how corporations are directed, managed, controlled and held accountable to their shareholders. In India, the question of Corporate Governance has come up mainly in the wake of economic liberalization and de-regularization of industry and business. The objective of any corporate governance system is to simultaneously improve corporate performance and accountability as a means of attracting financial and human resources on the best possible terms and of preventing corporate failure. With the rapid pace of globalization, many companies have been forced to tap international financial markets and consequently to face greater competition than before. Both policymakers and business managers have become increasingly aware of the importance of improved standards of Corporate Governance.

Definition of Corporate Governance

Definition of Corporate Governance varies widely. Corporate Governance could be defined as ways of bringing the interests of investors and managers into line and ensuring that firms are run for the benefit of investors. It is concerned with the relationship between the internal governance mechanisms of corporations and society's conception of the scope of corporate accountability. Corporate governance is the acceptance by management of the inalienable rights of shareholders as the true owners of the corporation and of their own role as trustees on behalf of the shareholders. It is about commitment to values, about ethical business conduct and about making a distinction between personal and corporate funds in the management of a company. Corporate Governance consists of procedures and processes according to which an organization is directed and controlled. The Corporate Governance structure specifies the distribution of rights and responsibilities among the different participants in the organization such as the board, managers, shareholders and other stakeholders and lays down the rules and procedures for decision-making. Corporate Governance is about promoting corporate fairness, transparency and accountability. In simple terms Corporate Governance can be defined as a set of laws, rules, regulations, systems, principles and processes by which a company is governed.

Need for Corporate Governance in India

A corporation is a congregation of various stakeholders, namely customers, employees, investors, vendor partners, government and society. In this changed scenario, an Indian corporation, as also a corporation elsewhere, should be fair and transparent to its stakeholders in all its transactions. This has become imperative in today's globalized business world where corporations need to access global pools of capital, need to attract and retain the best human capital from various parts of the world, need to partner with vendors on mega collaborations and need to live in harmony with the community. Unless a corporation embraces and demonstrates ethical conduct, it will not be able to succeed.

Corporations need to recognize that their growth requires the co-operation of all the stakeholders; and such cooperation is enhanced by the corporations adhering to the best Corporate Governance practices. In this regard, the management needs to act as trustees of the shareholders at large and prevent asymmetry of benefits between various sections of shareholders, especially between the owner-managers and the rest of the shareholders.

EVOLUTION OF CORPORATE GOVERNANCE

Scenario Abroad

The extraordinary events in corporate America during the last decade has renewed widespread, worldwide interest in corporate governance. The present crisis of confidence in corporate leadership owes its origin to the failures of seemingly – infallible corporations like Enron, Arthur Anderson, Tyco, Global Crossing, Adelphia and WorldCom. The recent US Mutual Fund problems have further added to the interest.

Public interest to corporate governance is nothing new – it dates back to the 1970s when, in the wake of the Watergate scandal legislation specifically mandating the establishment, maintenance and review of internal controls was passed in United States. Subsequently, in 1985, the Treadway Commission was formed following the savings and loan crisis. In the 1990s, the Cadbury Committee's code of best practices in the UK, the Combined Code of the London Stock Exchange, the Blue Ribbon Committee of the US, the OECD's code of 1998, and the joint efforts of the World Bank and the OECD's code to develop benchmarks in corporate governance have kept public interest kindling around the world.

Evolution of Corporate Governance in India

In India, while management processes were widely explored, till recently relatively little attention was paid to the processes by which companies were governed. The various aspects of this issue crept into India after the report of the Cadbury Committee in UK in 1992, which evoked considerable interest in Indian companies. The Confederation of Indian Industries (CII) thereafter published a Desirable Code of Corporate Governance, which some companies voluntarily adopted.

The issue came into prominence with the report of Shri Kumar Mangalam Birla Committee set by SEBI to suggest changes in the listing agreement to promote corporate governance.

Some companies voluntarily established high standards of corporate governance; however, there were many others who did not pay adequate attention to the interest of the shareholders. They did not attend to investors also who suffered on account of unscrupulous companies, which raised capital from the market at very high premium.

SEBI initiated several steps from strengthening corporate governance through the amendment of the listing agreement. However, SEBI continued to receive a large number of investor complaints daily. To further improve the level of corporate governance, it was felt that a more comprehensive approach was needed at that stage of development of the capital market. This prompted SEBI to constitute a committee under the Chairmanship of Sri Kumar Managalam Birla, to suggest changes in the Listing Agreement to promote Corporate Governance.

The Committee's report was made public. Based on the recommendations of the Committee and the feedback received, the SEBI Board at its meeting held on January 25, 2000 considered the recommendations of the Committee and decided to make amendments to the Listing Agreement in pursuance of these recommendations.

In August 2002, the Department of Company Affairs (DCA) under the Ministry of Finance and Company Affairs appointed a High Level Committee, under the Chairmanship of Naresh

Chandra, former Cabinet Secretary "to examine the Auditor-Company relationship, role of independent directors, disciplinary mechanism over auditors in the light of irregularities committed by companies in India and abroad".

In 2002, SEBI, having analyzed the disclosures made by companies under Clause 49 and after review of a large number of company's annual reports, observed that there was considerable variance in the extant and quality of disclosures made by companies in their annual reports and concluded that there was also a need to review the existing code on corporate governance to assess adequacy of existing practices and to suggest improvements to the existing practices. Thus, the SEBI Committee on Corporate Governance was constituted under the Chairmanship of N.R. Narayana Murthy to look into these matters.

The Narayana Murthy Committee Report, February 2003, reviewed existing best practices in corporate governance and also drew upon the recommendations of the Kumar Mangalam Birla Committee and the Naresh Chandra Committee to recommend further improvements in the existing system of corporate governance applicable to Indian companies.

In October 2004, SEBI amended Clause 49 of the listing agreement in alignment with the recommendations of the Narayana Murthy Committee. These changes primarily strengthened the requirements in the following areas:

(i) Broad composition and procedure
(ii) Audit Committee responsibilities
(iii) Subsidiary companies
(iv) Risk management
(v) CEO/CFO certification of financial and internal controls
(vi) Legal compliance
(vii) Other disclosures

Since large number of companies were not in a state of preparedness to fully comply with the requirements of the Revised Clause 49, it was felt that more time should be allowed to them, to conform to the provisions of the Revised Clause 49. Accordingly,

SEBI has extended the date for ensuring compliance with the Revised Clause 49 of the Listing Agreement to December 31, 2005.

Governance Practices and Regulations

The burgeoning economic growth that corporate India witnessed since the 1990s brought to the forefront the need for Indian companies to adopt corporate governance practices and standards, which are consistent with international principles. Industry groups, notably the Confederation of Indian Industries (CII), spearheaded the move to bring corporate governance issues to the attention of Indian companies and also led to the introduction of legislative reforms prescribing the manner in which Indian companies could implement effective corporate governance mechanisms.

The legal framework relating to corporate governance is broadly covered in the Indian Companies Act, 1956 (Companies Act) and the regulations/directives that are issued by the Securities and Exchange Board of India (SEBI), the securities market regulator in India. The Companies Act is administered by the Ministry of Corporate Affairs (MCA) and the provisions of the Companies Act are enforced by the Company Law Board. Regulators such as the Reserve Bank of India (RBI) and the Insurance Regulatory Development Authority (IRDA) also prescribe corporate governance guidelines applicable for banking and insurance companies, respectively.

The establishment of SEBI has also played a significant role in establishing norms for corporate governance in India. Over the years, SEBI constituted two committees to make recommendations relating to corporate governance in India, viz., the Kumar Mangalam Birla Committee (which submitted its report in 2000) and the Narayana Murthy Committee (which submitted its report in 2003). These committees made various recommendations relating to the composition of the Board of directors (Board) of listed companies, procedures for meeting of the Board, formation of an audit committee, disclosure of relevant information to the shareholders, etc.

Subsequently, the MCA also appointed the J.J. Irani Committee in 2004 to review the international best practices in corporate governance, in the light of the growing needs of the Indian economy and corporates. The recommendations of these committees form the bedrock of the legal regime for corporate governance in India. Legal and non-legal framework of corporate governance are provided in following paragraphs.

CORPORATE GOVERNANCE UNDER VARIOUS ACTS

Under the Companies Act

The fundamental principles of corporate governance have been enshrined in the Companies Act, which contains various provisions relating to shareholder rights, disclosure and transparency and Board responsibility. Some of the relevant provisions have been highlighted below:

(a) Shareholder Rights: The Companies Act requires every company to conduct an annual general meeting and provides an effective mechanism for the shareholders to participate and vote at general meetings. In the interests of investor awareness, the Companies Act also requires continuous dissemination of information to the shareholders in the form of a number of corporate documents such as annual reports, minutes of general meetings and Board meetings, auditor's report, Board's report, etc.

(b) Disclosure and Transparency Requirements: The Companies Act affirms that disclosure and transparency form an integral part of corporate governance and thus, information about the company and its activities has to be provided to the shareholders, registrar of companies and to the stock exchanges in the form of annual report and other corporate documents mentioned above. The annual accounts of the company are required to be certified by auditors, who are appointed at the general meetings.

(c) Responsibilities of the Board: The Board of a company is appointed at the general meeting, with each director's appointment to be approved by majority of the shareholders present and voting. Similarly, the shareholders can remove a director by way of simple majority of shareholders. The whole-time directors along with managing directors, managers, and secretary are classified as officers in default by the Companies Act. Even though the Board has general powers, consent of shareholders has been made mandatory for certain corporate decisions such as further issue of capital, issuing shares at a discount, buyback of shares, reissuing of redeemed debentures, change of registered office within the State and issuing of inter-corporate loans. The Companies Act also contains provisions safeguarding the interests of shareholders in the event of oppression and mismanagement in the company.

Corporate Governance Mechanism Prescribed by SEBI

SEBI, being the securities market regulator in India, has primary oversight on investor protection and its establishment played a significant role in establishing norms for the corporate governance in India. The SEBI Act, 1992 (SEBI Act) empowers SEBI to frame regulations, pursuant to which the regulator has introduced a comprehensive set of guidelines on insider trading, mergers and takeovers, fraudulent practices, etc., all of which have a significant impact on corporate governance in the country.

SEBI, as a market regulator, also decides the terms and conditions of listing agreement which govern the arrangement between stock exchanges and companies listed on the stock exchange. The listing agreement usually requires disclosures to be made by the company to the stock exchange. For instance, in terms of Clause 41 of the listing agreement, a company is required to submit quarterly financial results to the recognized stock exchange and these results are required to be approved by the Board of a company or by a committee (other than the audit committee). While doing this, the Chief Executive Officer and Chief Financial Officer of the company (by whatever name called), is required to certify that the financial results do not contain any 'false or misleading statement or figures and do not omit any material fact which may make the statements or figures contained therein misleading.' The corporate governance standards are elaborated in Clause 49 of the listing agreement.

Clause 49 of Listing Agreement

Clause 49 of the listing agreement is the most significant recent development in Indian legal regime relating to corporate governance. This clause, introduced in 2000 and subsequently revised, details the standards of corporate governance which every listed company is required to adopt and follow. Clause 49 of the listing agreement prescribes various corporate governance mechanisms in the following subject areas:

(a) Board of Directors and Independent Directors

The Board of a listed company is required to have an optimum number of executive and non-executive directors, with at least half of the Board comprising of non-executive directors. The clause defines an independent director and specifies the conditions which determine independence. Thus, the independent director is a person who:

(i) apart from director's remuneration, does not have any material pecuniary relationships or transactions with the company, promoters, directors, senior management or the holding company, subsidiaries and associates;

(ii) is not related to the promoters or persons occupying management positions at the Board level or at one level below the Board.

(iii) has not been an executive of the company for immediately preceding three financial years or who is not a partner or an executive or was a partner or an executive during the preceding three years, of the statutory audit firm, internal audit firm, legal firm, consulting firm associated with the company.

The independent director is also not permitted to be a substantial shareholder of the company, i.e., owns two per cent or more of the block of voting shares of the company.

With respect to the composition of the Board, Clause 49 mandates that at least one-third of the Board should comprise of independent directors, when the Chairman of the Board is a non-executive director or alternatively, at least half of the Board should comprise of independent directors, if Chairman of the Board is an executive director. Checks have also been placed on the scope of the power of directors by limiting the number of committees a director can be part of. Additionally, the listing agreement requires the company to adopt a code of conduct laid down by the Board, and ensure that such code is adhered to by the Board members and senior management of the company.

SEBI is also fairly vigilant of the activities of independent directors and in a recent case, has also held that independent directors can be held liable for the misleading and fictitious financial statements published by the company. While responding to the argument that independent directors are not involved or aware of the day-to-day functioning of the company, SEBI observed that "the institutions of independent directors and audit committee have been established to promote corporate governance and enhance the protection of interests of investors". The SEBI order also states that:

"While the extent of responsibility of an independent director may differ from that of an executive director, an independent director has a duty of care. This duty calls for exercise of independent judgment with reasonable care, diligence and skill which should be reasonably exercised by a prudent person with the knowledge, skill and experience which may reasonably be expected of a director in his position ....By failing to ask the right questions at the right point of time, I find that the persons have failed in their duty of care as an independent director."

(b) Audit Committees

The audit committee, which oversees companies' financial reporting process and necessary financial disclosures, is required to be helmed by an independent director. In order to ensure that the audit committee functions in an independent manner, two-thirds of the directors on the committee have to be independent directors.

(c) Subsidiary Companies

The presence of at least one independent director of the holding company, on the Boards of a material non-listed subsidiary company has been made compulsory by Clause 49. The financial statements, particularly investments made by the unlisted subsidiary company are also required to be reviewed by the above mentioned audit committee.

(d) Disclosures

Clause 49 of the listing agreement requires listed companies to make periodical disclosures of related party transactions, accounting treatment, risk management, remuneration of directors, management related matters, appointment and reappointment of directors and utilization of proceeds from public issues, rights issues, preferential issues etc.

(e) Report on Corporate Governance

A separate section, with a detailed compliance report on corporate governance, is required to be included in the annual reports of the company. A quarterly compliance report, as per the format in the listing agreement, is also required to be submitted to the stock exchange within 15 days from the close of quarter as per a specific format.

(f) Compliance

Lastly, the company is required to obtain an annual certificate from either the auditors or practicing company secretaries regarding compliance of conditions of corporate governance, which is then sent to the shareholders and stock exchanges.

Governmental Initiatives – Measures by Ministry of Company Affairs (MCA)

MCA is the executive arm which regulates the functioning of the corporate sector. It primarily administers the Companies Act and other allied acts, such as the Competition Act, 2002, Partnership Act, 1932, Companies (Donations to National Funds) Act, 1951 and Societies Registration Act, 1860. The MCA also exercises supervision over three separate bodies, established by the Parliament, concerned with the professions of Chartered Accountants, Company Secretaries and Cost Accountants respectively. As the primary government body, MCA has taken a number of steps in establishing the standards for corporate governance in the country. Some of the key initiatives taken by MCA are highlighted below:

(a) Voluntary Guidelines on Corporate Governance

MCA introduced the Voluntary Guidelines on Corporate Governance in 2009 ("Guidelines"), a set of best practices to develop ethical and responsible standards in the Indian industry. The Guidelines are completely voluntary in nature but are strongly recommended by the government to all public companies and large private companies as well. The guidelines relate to various issues such as: the constitution of Board (appointment, role of independent directors, remuneration); the responsibilities of the Board (training, enabling quality decision-making, risk management, evaluation of performance, compliance); audit committees of Board (constitution, enabling powers, role and responsibilities); and auditors (appointment, certificate of independence, rotation); secretarial audit; whistle blowers, etc.

(b) Green Initiatives

A number of green initiatives have also been recently introduced, such as: (i) service of documents through electronic mode to increase the speed of delivery, (ii) participation of directors and shareholders through video conferencing to provide larger participation and for curbing the cost borne to attend various meeting, (iii) secure electronic voting in the general meetings of the company and (iv) issuance of digital certificates and standard letters by the Registrar of Companies (ROCs) to reduce the delay.

(c) Serious Fraud Investigation Office (SFIO)

In 2003, SFIO was set up in the backdrop of stock market scams, failure of non-financial banking companies, phenomena of vanishing companies and plantation companies. The office investigates cases which have inter-departmental and multi-disciplinary ramifications or public interest at stake or the possibility of investigation contributing towards an improvement in systems, laws or procedures. The investigation is carried out only when it has been referred by the Central Government under sections 235 and 237 of the Companies Act.

(d) Investor Grievances Management Cell (IGMC)

IGMC, earlier known as the Investor Protection Cell, was set up by the MCA in 1993 with the objective of resolving the grievances of investors through the jurisdictional ROCs. IGMC coordinates with the RBI, SEBI and Department of Economic Affairs and broadly, deals with issues like non-receipt of annual report, non-receipt of dividend amount, non-refund of application money, etc. Recently, MCA has also permitted the use of MCA-21, an online portal, to receive grievances online.

(e) National Foundation for Corporate Governance (NFCG)

NFCG, the national apex platform on corporate governance issues, was established in 2003 by the MCA to act as a platform for deliberation on issues relating to corporate governance and sensitize corporate leaders on the importance of "good corporate governance, self-regulation and directorial responsibilities". Along with MCA, the other stakeholders in NFCG are Confederation of Indian Industry, Institute of Chartered Accountants of India, Institute of Company Secretaries of India, Institute of Cost and Works Accountants of India and National Stock Exchange of India Limited.

CHANGES ON THE ANVIL

The Companies Bill substantially reworked the framework of Companies Act and places greater emphasis on corporate governance norms and shareholder interests. Some of the key features of the Companies Bill have been highlighted below:

(i) The Companies Bill contains provisions relating to roles and responsibilities of independent directors, whose roles and responsibilities are currently featured only in Clause 49 of the listing agreement. Under the Companies Bill, one-third of the directors of a company are required to be independent directors.

(ii) The Companies Bill also proposed to empower the Central Government to prescribe minimum number of independent directors in case of public companies and subsidiaries of any public company which are not listed.

(iii) The Companies Bill recognizes the importance of disclosures in corporate governance and hence, provides for additional disclosures by the Boards such as disclosure relating to directors' remuneration, shareholding pattern, etc.

(iv) Additionally, the Companies Bill also proposes to introduce the concept of class action suits, which would empower member shareholders associations or group of shareholders to take legal action in case of any fraudulent action on the part of a company.

As is the case globally, even in India, compliance of corporate governance norms by a company is often a matter of subjective analysis and companies routinely have to face various practical constraints in implementing the applicable corporate governance framework. Clause 49 of the listing agreement, coupled with SEBI's regulatory oversight, continue to serve as the underpinnings of corporate governance in India.

STRUCTURE AND DEVELOPMENT OF BOARDS

The structure and composition of the board play a crucial role in the effective functioning of the board. Stakeholders and regulatory authorities are considering changes in composition of corporate boards to improve their functioning.

Directors can be categorized into various "types" depending on their relationship with the management of an organization. The different types of directors are:

- Executive directors
- Non-executive directors
- Nominee directors
- Representative directors
- Alternative directors
- Shadow directors

Executive Director performs a dual role as a member of the board of directors and as an executive in the organization. He is appointed as a director by the shareholders and, according to company law, is responsible to the shareholders like any other type of director. As an executive, he is an employee of the organization and is bound by an employment contract.

Non-executive Director is one who does not hold an executive position in the organization on whose board he works.

Nominee Directors are those who are appointed to the board of directors by the major stakeholders or financial institutions like banks, mutual funds, etc. These directors work towards safeguarding the interest of their principles. Even though external stakeholders like banks appoint them, they should act in the overall interest of the company.

Representative Directors are similar to nominee directors. They safeguard the interest of stakeholders groups like employees, customers etc. But they also act in the overall interest of the company.

Alternative Directors are appointed as per the Articles of Association to act as substitutes in absence of an original director. These alternate directors enjoy all the powers of the directors they represent on the board.

Shadow Directors are those who influence the decisions of the board without formally being present on the board. This type of directorship is seen in some family owned companies.

Issues in Designing a Board: Some of the issues that corporations should address designing a board structure are:

- The board size
- The role of the Chairman and the Chief Executive
- Duality in subsidiary company board

The Board Size: The company's Article of Association lay down the limit for thc number of directors to be present on its board. Some boards may have only two directors while other may have twenty or more directors. The size of the board generally depends on the size of the company, larger the company, larger the size of the board.

The role of the Chairman and the Chief Executive: Stakeholders and other regulatory bodies frequently ask corporations to separate the roles of the CEO and the Chairman. They see this as a pre-requisite to curtain the dominance of the CEO and to ensure balance of power on the board. However, most companies hold that in the present competitive environment, it is better for a company to have a single person playing the role of CEO and Chairman.

Duality in Subsidiary Company Board: Sometimes, executives from the parent company become non-executive directors on the board of a subsidiary. Clashes may occur between the executive directors of the subsidiary and the non-executive directors from the parent company, if there is a perception that the subsidiary is being used as a cash cow to finance the needs of other SBUs of the group.

ROLE OF CAPITAL MARKET AND GOVERNMENT

There has been efforts to improve the corporate governance by capital market and government for overall benefit of the economy and corporates. The dependence of corporates on capital markets needs no emphasis. Therefore, confidence building of investors on corporates plays in important role. Hence, the steps taken by capital market and government attain greater importance.

Liberalization and its associated developments, i.e., deregulation, privatization and extensive financial liberalization have made effective Corporate Governance very crucial. Cases of frauds and malpractices can render capital market reforms desultory. Independent and effective corporate governance reforms are, therefore, necessary in order to restore the credibility of capital market and to facilitate the flow of investment finance of firms. There are various reforms which were channeled through a number of different paths with both the Security and Exchange Board of India (SEBI) and the Ministry of Corporate Affairs, Government of India (MCA) playing important roles.

Given below are some of such efforts to improve the corporate governance by capital market and the government.

Committee on Corporate Governance

There are various committees formed with a view to reforming the Corporate Governance in India since 1990s. Some of the recommendations of these committees are highlighted below.

1. Confederation of Indian Industries (CII) set up a task force in 1995 under Rahul Bajaj, a reputed industrialist. In 1998, the CII released the code called "Desirable Corporate Governance". It looked into various aspects of Corporate Governance and was first to criticize nominee directors and suggested dilution of government stake in companies.
2. SEBI had set up a Commission under Kumarmanlagam Birla. This Committee covered issues relating to protection of investor interest, promotion of transparency, building international standards in terms of disclosure of information.
3. The Department of Companies Affairs (DCA) modified the Companies Act, 1956. It undertakes periodic review and brings about amendments in the Companies Act, 1956. In 1999, the Act introduced the provision relating to nomination facilities for shareholders and share buybacks and for formation of Investor Education and Protection Fund.
4. The Department of Corporate Affairs constituted Naresh Chandra Committee in 2002. The Committee talks extensively about the statutory auditor-company

relationship, rotation of statutory audit firms/partners, procedure for appointment of auditors and determination of audit fees, true and fair statement of financial affairs of companies.

5. SEBI appointed Narayana Murthy Committee in 2002. Its report mainly focuses on and makes mandatory recommendations regarding responsibilities of audit committee, quality of financial disclosure, requiring boards to assess and disclose business risks in the company's annual reports.

Clause 49 of the Listing Agreement

After liberalization, serious efforts have been made towards overhauling the system with SEBI formulating the Clause 49 of the Listing Agreements dealing with corporate governance.

Clause 49 of the Listing Agreement to the Indian stock exchange comes into effect from 31 December 2005. It has been formulated for the improvement of corporate governance. Steps taken through this measure is amply explained earlier. Though at the cost of repetition, it is worthwhile mentioning briefly the efforts here too since these are governmental efforts.

- **Board Independence:** Boards of directors of listed companies must have a minimum number of independent directors. Where the Chairman is an executive or a promoter or related to a promoter or a senior official, then at least one-half the board should comprise independent directors. In other cases, independent directors should constitute at least one-third of the board size.
- **Audit Committees:** Listed companies must have audit committees of the board with a minimum of three directors, two-thirds of whom must be independent. In addition, the roles and responsibilities of the audit committee are to be specified in detail.
- **Disclosure:** Listed companies must periodically make various disclosures regarding financial and other matters to ensure transparency.

- **CEO/CFO certification of internal controls:** The CEO and CFO of listed companies must: (a) certify that the financial statements are fair and (b) accept responsibility for internal controls.
- **Annual Reports:** Annual reports of listed companies must carry status reports about compliance with corporate governance norms.

Voluntary Guidelines Issued by Ministry of Corporate Affairs

Voluntary Guidelines on Corporate Governance were issued by the Ministry of Corporate Affairs in December 2009. Few guidelines are worth mentioning.

1. Board of Directors

Appointment of Directors Companies should issue formal letters of appointment to Non-Executive Directors (NEDs) and Independent Directors as is done by them while appointing employees and Executive Directors. Such a formal letter should form a part of the disclosure to shareholders at the time of the ratification of his/her appointment or reappointment to the Board.

- The offices of Chairman of the Board and Chief Executive Officer should be separate.
- The companies may have a Nomination Committee comprised of a majority of Independent Directors, including its Chairman. A separate section in the Annual Report should outline the guidelines being followed by the Nomination Committee and the role and work done by it during the year under consideration.
- Independent Directors and NEDs should hold no more than seven directorships.

Independent Directors

- The Board should put in place a policy for specifying positive attributes of Independent Directors such as integrity, experience and expertise, foresight, managerial qualities and ability to read and understand financial statements. Disclosure about such policy should be made by the Board in its report to the shareholders. Such a policy may be subject to approval by shareholders.

- All Independent Directors should provide a detailed Certificate of Independence at the time of their appointment, and thereafter annually. Independent Directors should be restricted to six year terms. They must leave for three years before serving another term, and they may not serve more than three tenures for a company.
- Independent Directors should have the ability to meet with managers and should have access to information.

Remuneration of Directors

- NEDs should be paid either a fixed fee or a percentage of profits. Whichever payment method is elected should apply to all NEDs. NEDs paid with stock options should hold onto those options for three years after leaving the board.
- Independent Directors should not be paid with stock options or profit-based commission.
- The Remuneration Committee should have at least three members with the majority of NEDs, and at least one Independent Director. Their decisions should be made available in the Annual Report.

2. Duties of the Board

- The Board should provide training for the directors.
- The Board should enable quality decision-making by giving the members timely access to information.
- The Board should put in systems of risk management and review them every six months.
- The Board should review its own performance annually and state its methods in its Annual Report.
- The Board should put in a system to ensure compliance with the law, which should be reviewed annually. All agenda items should be assessed for its impact on minority shareholders.

3. Audit Committee of Board

- The Audit Committee should be composed of at least three members, with Independent Directors in the majority and an Independent Director as the chairperson.
- The Audit Committee is responsible for reviewing the integrity of financial statements, the company's internal financial controls, internal audit function and risk management systems. The Audit Committee should also monitor and approve all transactions.

4. Auditors

- The Audit Committee should be consulted on the selection of auditors. The Committee must be supplied with relevant information about the auditing firm.
- Every auditor should provide a certificate stating his/her/its arm's length relationship with the client company.
- The audit partner should be rotated every three years; the firm should be rotated every five years. Audit partners should have a cooling off period of three years before they work with the client company again; the firm should have a cooling off period of five years
- The Committee may appoint an internal auditor.

5. Institution of a Mechanism for Whistle Blowing

- The companies should ensure the institution of a mechanism for employees to report concerns about unethical behaviour, actual or suspected fraud, or violation of the company's code of conduct or ethical policy.
- The companies should also provide for adequate safeguards against victimization of employees who avail of the mechanism, and also allow direct access to the Audit Committee Chairperson in exceptional cases.

Amendments in Companies Act

The Companies Bill 2009 is expected to be brought before Indian Parliament for consideration in the forthcoming Budget session. The provisions of the Companies Bill is related to eligibility, power and function of Auditor and Audit Committee, appointment and qualification of Directors, Independent Directors, meeting of the board and its power.

Efforts of MCA

The Ministry of Corporate Affairs (MCA) has issued two press releases on January 10, 2010 and January 22, 2010. The latter specifies the roadmap recommended by the Core Group set up by the MCA for Convergence of Indian Accounting Standards with IFRS.

The highlights of the roadmap include:

- Two sets of accounting standards (existing Indian Accounting Standards and Indian accounting standards converged with International Financial Reporting Standards (IFRS)).
- Indian accounting standards converged with IFRS would apply to specified class of companies in three phases.
- Existing Accounting Standards to apply to other companies (including Small and Medium Companies).
- Roadmap for Banking and Insurance companies to be announced by 28 February, 2010.

  Draft Companies (Amendment) Bill will be prepared by February 2010.

  Convergence of Accounting Standards to be completed by ICAI by 31 March, 2010 and NACAS to submit its recommendations to the Ministry by 30 April, 2010.

The amendment to Clause 49 was supplemented by efforts made by the Department of Company Affairs (DCA) and the Ministry of Financc (MoF) in enhancing the governance structure. The steps included the formation of the Naresh Chandra Committee on Corporate Audit and Governance in 2002, and the Expert Committee on Corporate Law (J.J. Irani Committee) in late 2004. The clear mandate was to provide more powers to the independent directors and audit committees. The Naresh Chandra

Committee proposed similar governance requirements like the Sarbanes Oxley Act, 2002 passed by the US Congress.

Auditor Independence

The Naresh Chandra Committee Report incorporated in Clause 49 also regulates the independence of auditors' process. The trend has been that most large companies use international auditing firms to audit their IFRS or US GAAP set of financial statements. However, there are a sizable number of Indian business houses which engage local accounting firms to audit their financial statements. With the inclusion of IFRS in the Indian statutory reporting framework, the auditing profession is likely to undergo a significant unlearning and relearning process to meet the challenges of the high quality financial reporting norms.

In nutshell, the World Bank's corporate governance assessment for India has shown that over the last few years, a series of legal and regulatory reforms have transformed the governance framework and significantly improved the level of responsibility and accountability of insiders, board and transparency. A giant step towards the endeavour was the Kumarmangalam Birla Committee Report, which led to the inclusion of Clause 49 in the listing agreement, in the year 2000. The second committee on Corporate Governance was under the Chairmanship of N.R. Narayana Murthy, formed in late 2002. Based on the recommendations of the second committee, SEBI issued a circular in 2003 revising Clause 49 of the listing agreement. The recommendations of the Committee included revisions to the independence of the Chairman and proportion of Independent Directors.

Clause 49 prescribed formation of an Audit Committee and a Shareholder Grievance Committee with independent directors representing two-thirds of the membership of the audit committee, and with at least one committee member possessing an expert knowledge in the field of finance and audit. Clause 49 also enhanced the disclosure requirements, including disclosure of compensation to non-executive directors.

SEBI has introduced the concept of IPO grading, done by a credit rating agency registered with SEBI, for all primary market issuers, who file their draft Red Herring Prospectus, on or after 1 May, 2007. The grading is performed after due consideration to governance structure and financial strength.

GOVERNANCE RATING

Concept of Corporate Governance Rating (CGR)

CGR is meant to indicate the extent to which a company adopts and follows such practices and conventions that would provide the stakeholders an assurance on the quality of Corporate Governance practices.

The CGR would indicate IRCR's current options on the relative level to which an organization accepts and follows the codes and guidelines of Corporate Governance Practices.

Features of CGR

It is mandate driven, not unsolicited. It is public rating disclosed only on acceptance. It is a confidential rating and company may accept and disclose only to select entities. It is accepted ratings subject to regular surveillance. It has exit option with a notice of 1 year.

Importance of CGR

CGR assists corporate to develop a credible opinion on its management quality and responsiveness towards the interests of all its financial stakeholders. Improved perception of investors may, in turn, influence a higher CGR rating and improve the comfort level of the statutory authorities and regulators. It can also be used as a check to determine the relative standing of the company with respect to the benchmarks of best corporate practices in the industry.

Linkage of CGRs with Credit Ratings

CGRs has some relationship but no direct linkage with credit rating. Credit rating is measured of credit risk, determinants are business outlook, competitive position, operational efficiencies and financial position. CGR is an assessment of management conduct and it is fair and transparent.

Thus, a high corporate governance rating does not necessarily imply high credit rating. Companies with high credit ratings are generally expected to have acceptable level of corporate governance

What CGR is Not?

CGR can affect the attractiveness of a company to potential investors (debt or equity), but CGR is not the following:

(i) CGR is not intended to be an opinion on:

- (a) Specific financial obligation
- (b) Capital market valuation
- (c) Future business outlook
- (d) Business competitiveness
- (e) Operational performance

(ii) CGR is not an audit.

(iii) CGR is not to be interpreted as an indicator of statutory compliance.

Parameters for Corporate Governance Rating

CGR is based on the core principles of corporate governance practices laid down by the business sector advisory group of OECD. These are fairness, transparency, accountability and responsibility. The codes and standards, which are applicable, have been defined in detail in the various committee constituted by the Securities and Exchange Board of India and the RBI.

The rating agency would consider these requirements and various parameters including those others:

- Ownership structure, i.e., shareholding structure
- Decision-making process

- Quality of information
- Management structure including board level issues
- Stakeholder relations
- Quality of financial reporting and other disclosures
- Financial discipline
- Fulfillment of interests of the financial stakeholders

Besides these broad parameters, the agency would evaluate number of sub-parameters for assigning CGRs.

ICRA's CGR Scale

CGR would fall between CGR1 indicating highest level of corporate governance in the Indian context to CGR 6 indicating poor level of corporate governance. Following are rating symbols and their implications:

- CGR1 – Highest level of corporate governance
- CGR2 – Highest level of corporate governance, but not as high as in CGR1
- CGR3 – Adequate level of corporate governance
- CGR4 – Moderate level of corporate governance
- CGR5 – Inadequate level of corporate governance
- CGR6 – Poor level of corporate governance

FUTURE OF GOVERNANCE – INNOVATIVE PRACTICES

Innovation in governance can be thought of as a system of mechanisms to align goals, allocate resources and assign decision-making authority for innovation, across the company and with external parties.

Setting Up of Centre for Good Governance

Some innovative practices can be found in governance in State governments. One of the strategic initiatives by Government of Andhra Pradesh, for improving governance was setting up of

Centre for Good Governance. It was formed in 2001 to provide analytical, research, and training backup to the reform effort. This helped to make several of the administrative reforms attempted in AP. These reforms included redefining the structures and functions of government bodies, re-engineering business processes in government to improve policy making and service delivery, much greater e-connectivity and greater use of e-governance, attempts to make the government more accountable, responsive, and transparent, big social development and antipoverty initiatives and anti-corruption and legal reforms. The Advisory Commission on People's Empowerment was formed in 2002. It made several recommendations. The implemented reforms include the following:

Performance Management System (PMS)

A governance-related PMS, can provide online invaluable information on the progress of the innumerable developmental programmes and projects conducted or funded by the government (on physical as well as financial indicators, and outcome indicators for social justice and other qualitative goals), the performance of various ministries and departments against Plan allocations, budgets and so forth, comparisons for the previous quarter, the previous year, etc. Such a system would strongly reinforce the accountability of department heads for performance, and facilitate appropriate rewarding of high performance that can turn the operating culture of the government from one of adherence to rules and regulations and expenditures to one of getting results.

In AP, government departments were classified into eight functional groups: economic development (primary sector); economic development (secondary and tertiary sectors); human development; welfare; local and urban bodies; infrastructure development; revenue generation; and governance (general administration, regulation, land records, law and order). A performance management system was adopted to monitor the progress of the eight types of government bodies. For this purpose, nearly 1000 performance indicators were developed for some 200 departments. A performance grading system was developed to grade functionaries and departments every month. The performance measured was not only in terms of outputs, but also processes like file disposal and days toured. An online performance tracking system was implemented that generated a number of reports. These reports were acted upon by decision-makers at the appropriate level.

Change Management Programme

A change management programme was instituted titled 'Governing for Results". For this, workshops were conducted for various departments that involved a SWOT (strengths, weaknesses, opportunities, and threats) exercise for each department and the development of action plans to improve functioning. Change agents were identified in each department and given training to push the reform agenda forward. Implementation of change agendas was monitored periodically by experts.

Innovation Units

Innovation units were set up in such key departments as education, health, welfare, agriculture, irrigation, industry, local self-government departments, and police. These units would support the development of reform action plan by the department.

Citizen's Charters

Citizen's Charter along the British pattern, was announced by about 90 departments with large public interfaces, and a system was being devised to monitor the implementation of these charters.

E-governance

Many initiatives were implemented in e-governance, an NPM tool that made AP a leader in this area. E-Seva offered 42 services to citizens under one roof, such as the payment of utility bills, issue of certificates and licenses, rail reservations etc. E-cops connected up police stations.

For the hinterland, an online system was set up to connect 16 government departments to rural citizens, to provide such services as information on land records and transactions. The Police Department also instituted a performance tracking system involving nearly a dozen indicators of performance of senior police functionaries. A system was being installed to automate various functions of government such as providing energy, higher education, finance, transport etc. To reduce corruption and delays the government set up e-procurement and a system for issuing driving licenses. During 1994 to 2002, some 100000 teachers were recruited through the use of information and communication technology, and not a single complaint or grievance was encountered.

Video Conferencing

Through satellite communications and wide area networks, the government harnessed communications technologies to facilitate video conferencing between the chief minister and district administrators, enable people to converse with the chief minister on a designated day, extension services for agriculturists, provide training programmes for disadvantaged groups, teleconferencing between top level functionaries, etc.

Outsourcing and Public-Private Partnerships

Outsourcing, involving public-private partnerships is another powerful NPM tool. Nearly a third of the civic services provided by the municipalities were outsourced to foster public-private partnerships. These included garbage disposal, de-silting of drains street lighting, maintenance of parks, finalization of accounts, and collection of advertisement tax. A scheme for self-assessment of property taxes due to the municipality was introduced in Hyderabad under which the city was divided up into valuation districts (valuation per square meter of construction). The rates were computerized and made accessible to the people, so that they could compute the tax due on their property and pay without bills being issued to them. Despite a steep reduction on the tax rate, the collections tripled between 1997-98 and 2002-03.

Single Window Clearance

A single window clearance scheme was launched in 2002 to process and provide various permissions required to set up an industrial unit. By August 2003, over 80 per cent of the approvals were issued within the prescribed time limits, and a further 3 per cent or so were deemed approvals because no rejection was made by the government before the prescribed time limits.

Similar innovations are done by other entities to improve the governance. There is lot of scope for innovation in governance both in corporate and governmental entities.

CHECK YOUR UNDERSTANDING

1. Explain the concept of corporate governance. What is the need for corporate governance?
2. Trace the evolution of corporate governance in India. What were the reasons for such development?
3. Do you agree that the legislations are adequate for corporate governance? Substantiate your views.
4. Explain the role of SEBI in improving the corporate governance. Are the steps effective enough?
5. What are the importance responsibilities cast on the board of directors with regard to corporate governance?
6. Narrate the efforts taken by the Government for implementing the corporate governance.
7. Explain the concept of governance rating. What are the parameters taken into consideration while doing the CGR?
8. Is there any scope for innovation in corporate governance? Cite some examples and explain.

REFERENCES

1. Fernando, A.C. : Business Environment, Pearson, Delhi.
2. Goyal, Alok Dr. and Mridula, Goyal: Business Environment, VK (India) Publication, New Delhi.
3. http://psrcentre.org/images/extraimages/312018.pdf